3/9/78

Jerry,

Because so many people
think so differently .... because
you are probably the most different
thinker .... I thought that you would
enjoy this book ....

Ken Bass

NOT
OF
ONE
MIND

NOT OF ONE MIND

DALE TARNOWIESKI

in cooperation with

Carla Graubard
Michael Sklaar
Richard Sikora
David Gilburd
Christopher Russo
Kristin Anundsen
Philip Henry
Rosalind Raia

amacom

A DIVISION OF AMERICAN MANAGEMENT ASSOCIATIONS

Library of Congress Cataloging in Publication Data

Main entry under title:
Not of one mind.
   Consists of answers to a survey conducted by American
Management Associations.
    1. United States—Social conditions—1960–
2. Businessmen—United States—Attitudes. 3. Social
problems. 4. Industry and state—United States.
I. Tarnowieski, Dale. II. Graubard, Carla. III. Amer-
ican Management Associations.
HN59.N645   309.1′73′092   76–2038
ISBN 0–8144–5416–X

First Printing

*For Cleveland
and
Georgia Brown,*

*Robert Flamholtz,
and
Joseph Ferrara, Jr.*

We want to say thank you to the more than 850 men and women who provided material for this book. This is your book more than ours, and we hope that in editing some of your comments for publication we have done no injury to what you wanted to say.

We also want to express our sincere appreciation to the staff and management of AMACOM and the American Management Associations for your support and many contributions to this book. Special thanks are due Susan Eno, Beata Gray, and Robert Silver.

Finally, a very special note of thanks to Harvey Berger, Bruce Barton Bergquist, Caroline Cannon, Barbara Daley, Steven Gottesman, Ralph and Judy Heller, Wayne Lavender, Ph.D., David McCreary, Timothy McInerney, Glenn Matthews, Linda Reiman, George Renz, William Rippner, Dennis Siple, and Thomas O. Yancey, Jr., for your ideas, effort, love, and encouragement.

ACKNOWLEDGMENTS

CONTENTS

We used two methodologies in conducting research for this book. First, we compiled material gathered from scores of casual conversations and from a few formal interviews with men and women in business and industry, education, government, and other walks of life. Some of the people with whom we talked were self-employed professionals with past or present organizational ties—and a few were *un*employed at the time we spoke with them. Altogether, more than 100 people contributed in this manner.

Another 769 men and women provided *written* commentaries in response to one or more of 13 essay questions we put to them in writing in late 1974 and early 1975. Nearly all of these participants were members of the American Management Associations at the time we corresponded.

Altogether, the participants in the nationwide inquiry provided more than 1,400 separate statements in response to the questions and just under 2,000 pages of handwritten or typewritten comment. Replies to the questions ranged in length from a word or two to more than ten handwritten pages. A few returns were accompanied by printed matter such as religious tracts, newspaper and magazine clippings, or other types of previously published material. Survey participants and individuals interviewed were guaranteed anonymity, and no names of individuals or organizations have been used here in connection with the presentation of interview- or survey-based material.

A number of our questions probed philosophical attitudes, while most were more down to earth. Two questions that called for particularly personal responses received the fewest replies. Some participants had very complimentary things to say about the questionnaire, while others found fault with the questions or were critical of the study in general.

"These are provocative questions," one participant wrote, "that will lead some readers into uncomfortable realms of memory and contemplation. A lot of illusions about our country and the democratic process have been shattered in recent years. More than a few dreams have gone down the drain. A lot of nerves are on edge now. The restoration of confidence in many aspects of our system will be a long and painful experience for some Americans. Others may never quite believe in the system again. Questions like yours are useful and compelling—but damn if they don't hurt! Nevertheless, congratulations to AMA. Do more of this."

BASIS OF THE RESEARCH

An account executive (and vice president) with a Pennsylvania insurance broker-age firm was annoyed by the questionnaire and said that his first reaction was to throw it into the wastebasket. "My mind is still simple enough," he added, "to believe that the vast majority of the American public believes and has full faith in the American system of politics and business. Over the years we have had our 'ups' and 'downs,' but the 'plus' is the big thing. I believe that you and I and our organizations should tell the world of our great accomplishments—politically, so-cially, and financially. Let's reverse any negative attitudes toward our country. It is still and will be the best there is."

Another respondent *may* have thought our questions were suggesting we write *finis* to the American experience: "I have no concern that we are headed toward social bankruptcy or that this nation will fall," a Missouri food manufacturing executive asserted. "The current problems of energy, corrupt government, and crime will pass from the critical scene and we will handle them in the course of demand. We are not a Roman Empire destined to fall, but, as a pluralist society, we will continue to coexist with problems as they occur."

The executive vice president of a Texas company in the electronics services field said that he hoped "AMA takes the responses from this survey and uses them, not only to educate management—or merely to provide a lengthy report to management—but also to communicate with the American people." Another par-ticipant, a professional from Indiana, wanted to know what the problems of Amer-ican society had to do with American business and business management, while the treasurer of a New Hampshire firm asked why the American Management Associa-tions didn't just "stick to its middle name." The general manager of a company in Colorado asked why the researchers were "on a fishing expedition looking for trouble. I believe in the precepts of the Holy Bible," he added. "Most all of your questions seem to carry an implication of trouble that I don't subscribe to."

Another participant from middle America wrote this lengthy comment: It is "time for organizational management to rethink its relationship and responsibilities to the larger society. Specifically, I believe that too many businessmen think of business as an institution that *is* or *ought to be* free to operate pretty much as it pleases as long as it continues to produce the goods and services demanded by society. For some of the 'boys upstairs' business is a big competition game—a *deadly* sport for some—to one-up or out-do the other fellow or the other company. The result of this kind of thinking and behavior has been a lot of waste—a waste of time, money, materials, and worst of all, a waste of human talent and human lives. A few executives I'm acquainted with believe that this nation should be just plain grateful—no questions asked!—for what American industry has done for it. They don't understand, for example, what the consumer movement is all about today. A few are really out of touch with reality. A few have forgotten that coming to terms with reality is not a matter of changing reality—it's a matter of changing *their* outlook. For me, your questions call uneasy attention to so much that is disturbing in America today. I am very pleased to see that AMA is not afraid to raise these kinds of issues among businesspeople."

This note of disapproval came from a manager in a California personnel services agency: "I suspect," the respondent wrote, "that the fool who created this project knows that the people who think the United States has gone to hell and want to prove it will be those who, doing nothing useful anyhow, will have the time to answer. I'm surprised that AMA takes the time of working managers and busi-nessmen on this crap."

"You are inviting us to play 'Ain't It Awful' in transactional analysis terms," the vice president of personnel for a New York state utility company charged. "Not very professional. I decline to play, and question the use of AMA funds.'' From Ohio, the managing partner of an engineering consulting firm said he thought that collectively our questions reflected ''a 'bad-mouthing' and 'downgrading' of our country, our society, and our political and business life which is far from warranted. We do have our defects, but these can be rectified by reinstilling the work ethic, respect for person and property, and a dedication to fair play—the Golden Rule.''

An Illinois attorney and apparel manufacturing executive wrote that he deplored ''the whining negativism with which each of the questions is colored. The confidence, satisfaction, and strength which have grown in America and Americans of all ages and circumstances during the 1930–1974 years cannot be expressed in the responses these dismal questions will elicit.''

Another participant who asked to remain completely anonymous had more favorable things to say about the research instrument: ''I don't believe I've seriously thought about what life means to me in many years now. But a person's ideas about the meaning and purpose of life are relevant to so much—to his self-esteem; to his relations with family, friends, and business associates; and to his (or her) work and life goals in general. Your questions are powerful and have caused me to sit back and take stock for a moment in the life I'm living. This has been a very beneficial experience for me. Thanks for including me in your mailing.''

The director of marketing services for an upstate New York firm wrote the following in a letter to AMA: ''I am distressed by the questionnaire and its construction. The questions are leading, obviously pointing up an individual's point of view. I disagree completely with his point of view. I can't for the life of me understand what the motives are. I am surprised that AMA would sponsor such a survey. I would hope that your membership refuses to answer. I would certainly think that you might investigate the motives of those responsible.''

Finally, a number of respondents—and most of the people interviewed—expressed a simple ''thanks'' for the opportunity to express their views on matters of national concern. Some felt that organizational management would profit by involving itself more with these kinds of matters—especially in view of the increasing pressure on business and other institutions to behave more responsively. ''It is no longer enough,'' one participant told us, ''for companies to merely 'mind their own business.' ''

Our purpose in doing this book is to create a vehicle through which a large number of men and women who manage or work in organizations can share with all of us their thoughts about the national condition and the meaning and purpose of life in America on the eve of our national bicentennial. In fact, more than 850 people—representing a broad spectrum of organizational life and functional responsibilities—contributed material for this book.

We believe that the voices on the pages that follow are representative of a broad profile of managerial thinking in America. With few exceptions, these are not the voices of *national* opinion-makers. No attempt was made to solicit elite points of view or to limit participation in the study to individuals having greater weight as national spokespeople.

Some of the statements included here seem easy enough to comprehend, while others may be more difficult to follow. Here and there, it may be necessary to look beyond the words to see their meaning; here and there, it may be necessary to read this book between the lines.

Some of the voices reflect confidence and optimism—some, complacency or indifference. Some speak to us in terms of new visions of tomorrow, while others seem to mourn the passing of the good old days and wish that life could be the way it was again. Some ask us to accept the inevitability of change, and a few seem to come from other worlds of more rigid notions. Some of the comments flow mainly from emotion, while others reveal a more intellectual approach to life and its experiences. But one person's meat is another's poison, and we have not made it our task here to pass judgment.

This study is not a *conclusive* work. Instead, it is like a picture puzzle from which many of the pieces are missing. But we feel that the picture outlined here is complete enough to show that (among American managers and other professionals) the psychological state of the union is marked by a broad diversity of outlook and opinion on the eve of the national bicentennial.

Based on the material included here, we feel we cannot support the contention of some observers that managers in business are the mindless servants of the Corporate State. The statements of belief that follow seem to us proof enough that American

A FEW WORDS TO BEGIN WITH...

management is not of one mind: it inhabits a very large house filled with many rooms, and what seem to be self-evident truths to some people are sharply disputed by others—in social priorities, personal values, and life expectations generally.

It is not *our* purpose to suggest, through this book, what our national priorities and social objectives ought to be. Nor are we suggesting that the ideas presented here reflect *all* the value and belief systems that exist in our society today. Moreover, the opinions voiced here may not be proportionately representative of the thinking and values of American management or of the American people as a whole. There is no claim and no evidence that they are. But most of the people whose words comprise most of the text are men and women in positions of authority and responsibility in American business, education, government, and other institutional settings that make up the framework of our society and that influence millions of us in our day-to-day thinking and behavior (and emotional states, as well). Their voices, then, are not *in*consequential.

This study is a *presentational* work—a collection of some of the thoughts that some of those who manage the "system" are thinking about the national and human condition today and about our society's prospects for the future. No doubt, this work has been influenced to some extent by our own natures and experience—but not enough, we trust, to compromise what our many coauthors have wanted to say.

We have made no effort to interpret what all the viewpoints presented here *mean* in the aggregate. In fact, if the words that follow can tell us something about ourselves, our society, our values and beliefs, and our reasons for living, let each reader find his or her own meaning and draw his or her own conclusions.

Dale Tarnowieski

When we* were invited to comment for this book, two questions, in particular, prompted many of us to respond. The first asked us to talk about what disappointed us most about life in our country today. The second asked that we identify and discuss those forces at work in America today that we believe pose the greatest threat to our society and our way of life. The researchers wanted to know how we thought we might best deal with these threats—individually, collectively, or both. To what extent, they asked, were we personally concerned for the future well-being of our social, economic, and political arrangements? Is the bottom really falling out of the barrel, as some commentators would have us believe?

The forces at work in our society today that trouble or alarm us are many and varied. Many challenge some of our most time-honored ideas and institutions. Some will necessitate critical choices that will not be easy to make.

While Watergate, to begin with, served to focus national attention on our country's political and governmental processes, we are troubled today by far more than the corrupt or deceitful behavior of some of those in high places elected or appointed to serve us. There is a widespread consensus among us that the scope and influence of government at all levels pose as great a danger to our national well-being as do the dishonesty and lawlessness of some of our politicians and bureaucrats.

In more specific terms, we are troubled by a lack of effective leadership at all levels and in all branches of our government; by a free-spending philosophy that has led to higher taxes and a burgeoning bureaucracy; by the disproportionate influence wielded by special interest groups, minorities, and other activists; by a host of social welfare programs that seem to many of us to have created more problems than they have solved; by a steady erosion of democratic process and a steady drift away from constitutional government; by the failure of our courts to honor the law and to adequately punish those guilty of breaking it; by growing public apathy, on the one hand, or public expectations, on the other, that exceed the capacity of our institutions—our government, in particular—to deliver. Many of us believe that people expect too much from government today—and that government unwisely expects too much of itself.

1

THE AMERICAN CONDITION

---

* Introducing each chapter, and interspersed within chapters, are comments that might be called "the theoretical collective voice" of all of the respondents—thoughts of the participants in this study, presented as if they themselves were speaking directly to us. —D. T.

Our major threat is big government and free-spending social programs that lead to hyper-inflation and blunt individual incentive and capacities. Since FDR, the American people have been deluded into believing that government can spend more than it takes in in revenues. The end result is bankruptcy for any individual who lives this way—and the same is true for a country as well. With a country, it just takes longer.

Director of publishing services (40 to 49), publishing company, Maryland

The growing, undisciplined, untrained, biased encroachment of government on business and people is the biggest threat to our society. For example, government agencies push safety and environmental causes which lead to an increase in the cost of doing business. Then, products don't sell because they are too expensive, and the economy is threatened. This leads to more government action to control the economy, and the forces of the marketplace cannot operate naturally. So everyone is hurt by too much government.

Personnel manager (40 to 49), transportation company, Virginia

There is too much government influence in America today. People would be appalled if they knew the extent of government control on business. This condition worsens as government grows and grows. My personal concern is that individualism and laissez-faire are rapidly disappearing in our country today.

Personnel director (40 to 49), mining company, Georgia

The law—which is the cornerstone of the American way of life—threatens our nation's stability. Since the sole purpose of Congress is to create new laws, it is inevitable that more and more laws will be created. The system is self-generating. The more laws we get, the more lawyers we need. The more lawyers we have, the more laws we get. Laws are aimed at the governed rather than at those who govern. This tends to restrict individual liberty and to increase the power of government controls. The increasing number of laws increases the number and size of regulating agencies. This results in a reduction in the number of people producing goods and services. Two out of three components of our government deal with laws. No component of government deals with the elimination of laws. The Supreme Court is a reactive body that only deals with cases brought before it. Our courts are severely backlogged, business is strangling, and individual liberty is at stake. The American system of checks and balances is out of balance. A proactive body is needed to provide a positive rather than a restrictive mode of government with law the cornerstone rather than the bars of the American way of life.

Management development manager (50 to 59), manufacturing company, Virginia

The greatest single threat to the American way of life today is the growth in the philosophy—among government officials and educators—that this country owes us a living. We cannot survive with this philosophy. Each individual in America must do something for himself or herself and not wait for the government to take care of them. If people want to do good, let them do it at their own expense and not at the government's expense.

Personnel manager (50 to 59), manufacturing company, Massachusetts

Federal government deficit spending is the greatest threat to our society today. In my opinion, we need a constitutional amendment to require a balanced budget each year for federal government operations and programs—one that outlaws deficit spending. All citizens can insist that their Congressmen work for such an amendment. I am very concerned about the future well-being of our society. I don't believe the bottom is falling out of the barrel, but we are setting the stage for that to happen in the not-too-distant future.

Assistant commissioner (30 to 39), state agency, Virginia

The greatest threat to the American way of life today is our desire to overcome everything objectionable. Ecologists advocate a perfect world at the expense of eliminating jobs and wasting raw materials. We are now restricting our population growth to a point where there is a vacuum of people in the under-5 age group. We have a population that will be heavily weighted to senior citizens in 20 years. Politicians are advocating that everything be done in the full exposure of the press and the world, while European and Asiatic countries plot behind the scenes. Every organization is being attacked—the FBI, the CIA, the military, the presidency. Look what happened to the economy after Nixon went! We are being torn apart by some internal pressure which no one recognizes. It will probably take a war to restore us to our equilibrium.

Vice president, manufacturing (50 to 59), packaging company, South Carolina

Our gravest problem is the huge and growing government bureaucracy. It has done damage and is continuing to do damage to our nation because of (1) its size (one out of every six people works for the government and the rest of us must carry the load); (2) the destruction of the materialistic (capitalistic) drive through tax laws, controls, mass spending, monetary policies, over-legislation, and huge welfare programs; (3) public protection laws and a penal system that is too liberalized; and (4) a public education system into which too much "liberalism" has been inserted.

President (30 to 39), construction company, Florida

Before commenting on the greatest threat to our way of life, we ought to establish what our way of life is. I believe that the thing which distinguishes our way of life from that of other cultures is the original idea of limited government and a free market. So identifying the greatest internal threat to our way of life is simple: *activists*. Activists of many political viewpoints who don't like those features of our way of life have met and are meeting with great success in reducing individual freedom and increasing government. There is actually less and less of a distinctly American way of life in these areas. Everyone knows that government is getting too big, costing too much money, increasing the problems it allegedly tries to alleviate, and is heading toward a Big Brother type of total power. The income tax, compulsory safety and health programs, and all the regulatory agencies are examples of government excess.

Social studies instructor (30 to 39), Wisconsin high school

Our biggest danger is government intervention and control. In order for the labor unions to pressure companies to provide benefits to employees who were not earning them, the unions became active in politics and have been successful in getting laws passed and enforced on a biased basis. This way of running things has been in effect for such a long time that our younger people (along with some older ones) assume that government control and regulation is the answer to all problems. The real key to a turn-around is *less* government. Let the free enterprise system work! Also, the news media has in so many cases distorted the facts that it is now essentially impossible to educate and properly inform the masses in what is really happening to our great country. I am trying to fight back by participating more in politics and, to a lesser extent, in education.

Executive (50 to 59), mining and milling company, Idaho

Our way of life is threatened by the lack of responsible leadership in the federal legislative branch. There is a similar situation at the state level. Moreover, I have real concern for the inability of the American people to adapt to "less of everything" and to tighten their belts. There is also a lack of desire on each individual's part to achieve higher productivity. Perhaps our forefathers were correct in their belief that only the well-to-do and the landowners should establish policy.

Financial manager (under 30), electric utility, Florida

Our biggest problem is the inability of politicians in our country to honestly deal with the problems affecting us. We need to get rid of politicians who live in a dream world and/or use their positions for self-betterment or the betterment of their friends. The bottom has fallen out. We can only go up.

Assistant vice president (30 to 39), New York bank

The only sense of pride left in us Americans is in the idea that our system is the best in the world even with all its troubles. Yet, deep down inside every American is bewilderment over our "sissy" methods and use of power and force and over the rape of our treasury by inefficient, ineffective, incompetent politicians who manage statistics and make decisions on the basis of what will please rather than serve mankind.

President (50 to 59), Texas company

Our greatest internal threat is the increasingly pervasive belief on the part of our citizenry that we can have our cake and eat it too—that increasing our debts and printing more money will somehow cure the ills of our faltering economy. Not unlike the Roman politicians who provided bread and circuses from the public treasury, our state and national politicians provide matching funds to local governments, support wild-eyed socialistic experiments based on political expediency, and ever more richly reward indolence. If the money is not available for these purposes, more is printed or borrowed. Unless all of us—individually, locally, regionally, and nationally— make the necessary sacrifices and adjustments to balance our budgets and pay as we go, the bottom will indeed fall out of the barrel.

Executive (50 to 59),
electric utility, Washington

The greatest threat to our way of life is the greed and lust for power on the part of our elected representatives. I would like to see more women in positions of power. But the problem is not just with our present leaders. It's the things that happened in the past that must also be exposed—come what may. Only then can we start to clean house. Another problem is that we try to buy friends. Millions have been spent and look where we are today.

Supervisor of career and
educational counselors (50 to 59),
U.S. government, Maryland

Our political and social problems are not being handled properly. Our politicians are getting to be less and less concerned about the free enterprise system. But there is no such thing as a "free lunch," and there is far too much influence being wielded today in our political and social activities by lawers, college professors, and "eggheads."

Executive vice president,
marketing (50 to 59),
Pennsylvania company

The complexity of life grows exponentially due in small part to technology and in large part, it seems, to governmental regulation. Politicians venture to control things that are often better left alone, because the general public doesn't understand and politicians consider it the popular thing to do. This process sometimes works in reverse. In short, the best thing to do politically in terms of better management for the most becomes a cop-out for popularity. President Ford will not

DISAPPOINTMENTS WITH AMERICA

My greatest disappointment with the American way of life is the general helplessness on the part of most people to be able to do anything to change things for the better. Government, for another thing, has become too big at all levels and remains unresponsive to the will of the people.

Head of systems division
(50 to 59), New York company

People aren't satisfied with our way of life. They are pessimistic about the future. We have the greatest way of life. Yet the news media play up the disappointments and problems until everyone is pessimistic.

President (30 to 39),
building materials
distribution company, Montana

My greatest disappointment and concern today has to do with the rapidly increasing control the government (mostly federal) is exercising over all aspects of our daily lives—personal as well as corporate. As a nation of supposedly "free entrepreneurs" this course would seem to be counterproductive to the health and continuation of our system and the wealth it has brought our people. Hand-in-hand with these concerns is the ever-increasing percentage of our total national income that is spent for government at all levels.

President (50 to 59),
candy manufacturing
company, Pennsylvania

My single greatest disappointment with the American way of life is our tremendous dependency on material possessions for our happiness. We are energy and raw material gluttons, and it is now evident to me that we will be forced to cut back on our use of both. Unfortunately, the few leaders of our country who seem to understand this situation are not sufficiently influential, politically and socially, to create the necessary understanding of the problem among our people.

President (60 or over),
newspaper advertising sales
company, Connecticut

What disappoints me most about life in our country today is the lack of honesty in people, the increase in crime, and the lack of respect we show for others.

Vice president, corporate planning (50 to 59), manufacturing company, Illinois

My father used to say, "All is not as it appears." Today, nothing is as it appears. Everyone has an angle, from the factory worker who demands more than he contributes and the politician who wants his name in the history books to the preacher who wants a new church—or, more likely, a new parsonage. Laws have proliferated to a point that there is a high probability that each one of us is a criminal at some time or another during each day. Considering the likelihood of getting caught, getting convicted, and receiving any significant degree of punishment, there is probably a greater risk in going into business today than in robbing a bank.

Administrator and instructor (50 to 59), postsecondary educational institution, Michigan

It seems to me that a combination of factors has led to the world being out of control. These factors are the sheer size of our population, the high rate of change, and nontraditional forces in the economy. The people trying to cope with the situation are traditionalists (trying to use economics that are 20-plus years old and thus outdated) who are not by training or by nature the kind of people able to cope with rapid change—let alone to control it. In the United States today this situation is further aggravated by the total lack of leadership and statesmanship exhibited by government officials during the past six years at a time when leadership by the United States has been sorely needed—and indeed expected—by many other nations.

Vice president (50 to 59), chemical company, New Jersey

My biggest disappointment with America is the gradual erosion of individual incentive to grow, prosper, and excel. In other words, we are turning both ends of the spectrum toward the middle. "We won't let you be poor and neither will we let you be rich. You must conform."

General manager (50 to 59), woodwork manufacturing company, Iowa

There is far too much influence invested in the Pentagon. Let's strive rather for a better ratio of doctors and dentists to general population, as our "backward" European cousins enjoy. Let's siphon more of our dollars into medical research and development for the betterment of humanity rather than into the military for the machines of human destruction.

Assistant treasurer (60 or over), retail catalog showroom chain, Tennessee

The free enterprise system to which we owe so much is no longer free. The massive growth of government control and intrusion into the normal workings of a free market system has negated and frustrated our national economy. The urge to control everything is an extension of society's efforts to protect itself from real criminal acts through a legal and judicial system. The trouble is that we've gone too far. Now people, still seeking a mother or father to take care of them, expect their government to give them every security they need or think they need. All of us forget that a government can't give anything that it hasn't first taken away. The total effect of having had it so good has softened the character of most of us. The real hardships of the pioneers and those who suffered through economic depressions made the United States what it is today. Only an understanding of real values and a willingness to be more self-sufficient as individuals will improve our situation. More bureaucracy and economic manipulation can only worsen it.

President (50 to 59), chemical manufacturing company, Illinois

take positive action to prevent another fuel crisis; congressmen are sponsoring legislation against remarking prices without giving adequate consideration to turnover rates, rising costs, etc. There are so many examples of our legislative managers knuckling under to populist demands without considering all of the factors necessary for objective action.

Supervising engineer (30 to 39), engineering company, New York

The greatest threat to our country is the idea that government should do everything. Our democratic way of life and our free enterprise system will be destroyed. Government is elected on the basis of promises made and actions taken to stay in office. Political decisions must override what is best for the country. The decisions required to reduce inflation and prevent anarchy cannot be made under our popular vote system of electing officials to make those decisions. The socialistic concept of making everyone equal by spreading the wealth destroys initiative—institutional and individual.

Personnel manager (40 to 49), pharmaceutical company, Texas

The greatest danger confronting us is our inability to elect representatives to public office that are dedicated to the good of the country rather than to minority groups that elect them. Another problem is our inability to control government spending. Once a spending program is launched, it can never be shut off. We are also giving away massive foreign aid that the voters know nothing about, and who knows how much of it goes to the needy? Don't we ever wonder why every country in the world—including Canada—hates us?

Banker (50 to 59), Michigan

The greatest threat we face is the willingness of government to follow the thinking of the electorate rather than to lead the electorate to intelligent conclusions that will keep our nation strong. Our leaders need to speak out on the need to develop and pursue national goals. Ronald Reagan plans to do this in 1975. I believe that unless leadership is brought forward we may wind up with an unintelligent and irresponsible government that will be around for a long time. The bottom is falling out of the barrel, but it can be stopped through effective leadership by influential people who are able to influence all strata and segments of our society.

Administrative services manager
(50 to 59), Texas company

The greatest threat we face is that posed by special interest groups concerned with what benefits them regardless of the effect their actions have on society as a whole. Also, it seems to me that we are teaching our children and young adults that laws, rules, regulations, etc., are for others. We must deal with both these threats individually and collectively. We must be more willing to compromise and to give up short-range personal or group benefits so as to achieve long-range benefits for society. This will result, I believe, in individual and group benefits that are better for the country in the long run. We must also restore respect for authority and create this respect by our words and deeds. However, authority must also behave in a manner deserving of our respect.

Marketing manager (30 to 39),
consulting firm, Texas

We are threatened by the manner in which many of our institutions are caving in to the tyranny of the "minorities." No longer is the democratic process valued. It seems that we must now stack the deck to ensure the participation or representation of this group or that race or one sex or another. Soon, it appears, we will have to do the same for religious groups. Thus, the will of the majority is constantly being thwarted by mis-

guided efforts to make amends for past hurts or discrimination. The result is a thoroughly rigged deal which has no more merit than Watergate!

Personnel director (40 to 49),
state university branch
campus, Maryland

The biggest danger to America is in the political arena in Washington where our senators and congressmen have been joining in protests and encouraging others to do the same at the expense of the American way of change—an orderly process involving the exercise of the right to vote. Most members of Congress and congressional aspirants are so negative and take no positions on how to improve our national situation. We have lost sight of working to earn a living and to accumulate wealth. We give too much away to nonworkers. This has caused the United States to become weak. We are no longer the world leader we should be and were.

Industrial relations director
(40 to 49), record
company, California

The single greatest threat to the American way of life (and the American Dream) is the U.S. government. Through its power to tax, it is destroying the traditional American Dream that hard work can achieve objectives. In reality, present U.S. policies have placed the American middle class in a state of economic serfdom from which it will be difficult to escape. The harder one works, the more one advances and earns, the more the government takes away. Today, working people may have less than those who do not work and who are the recipients of government hand-outs. Industry, thrift, integrity, and character count for little in government and business today. Present-day American life no longer represents something to work for as far as I'm concerned, but something to be avoided and resisted by both me and my family.

Research writer (50 to 59),
Minnesota

The biggest threat to America today is the burgeoning number of people who are being placed on government payrolls (at the local, state, and national levels) in addition to all those who are already on the public payroll or who are receiving pay for not working and producing. The burden is becoming too great for the producers to bear, yet demagogue politicians continue to play to the so-called consumers who are, in fact, a mob that doesn't understand that someone, somewhere, must work, plan, invest, and produce to pay for all of this. The answer is to cut all government payrolls at the same rate that we cut other payrolls during a recession. Also, we should stop providing food stamps to people under 65 years of age who are able-bodied and do not have children to support. In fact, this should apply to all types of welfare with the exception of unemployment compensation for people who have been laid off.

Public and industrial relations director (40 to 49), beef producing company, Colorado

Our total government has gotten away from the Constitution of the United States. We could best deal with this by going back to doing what is best for the most people instead of our present policy of doing what is best for the minority that is loudest. I don't believe that the bottom is falling out of the barrel, but the government is shoving it out through excessive spending and taxation.

Industrial engineering manager (30 to 39), manufacturing company, Indiana

This nation is now ruled by a handful of industrialists and power brokers in a two-headed political system. The system has degenerated to a state of fascism that can only lead to more repression and greater exploitation of the citizenry. The threat to our well-being can only be countered by a revolution similar to that which is now occurring in China. I am deeply concerned for

the future. This is the only life I and my family will ever have. I contribute to improving the situation in every way I can. If I have anything to do with it, the bottom will fall out of the barrel we're in.

Administrative analyst (30 to 39), city of New York

Welfarism is the greatest threat to our country today and has been for years. The "womb to tomb" concept has destroyed any motivation among the masses to improve the quality of life. If we are going to better our collective lot, every individual must do his share.

Director (60 or over), state agency, Pennsylvania

We have converted a country founded in 1795 on the basis of a franchised voting republic into a democracy. The concept of a democracy was rejected then because this form of government sinks to the level of the masses, to the lowest level. In 1795 (and until recently) no resident of Washington, D.C., could vote, because originally Washington, D.C., was the federal district. As the federal district, Washington residents had a vested interest. Ergo—no vote! In 1795, a person had to be a citizen (no Indians, no slaves, no foreigners) and a property owner ($20 of chattels) to vote. Today, any illiterate, indigent person on welfare—as well as anyone on city, state, and federal payrolls—can vote. Obviously, we vote for the same "free wheat and free circuses" program that was designed to continue the Roman Empire for 5,000 years after Caesar.

Chief executive officer (40 to 49), insurance company, Louisiana

The biggest threat to our way of life is socialism in the United States today. This is based on the theory that big government in Washington is necessary and the answer to all our problems. I am not concerned with com-

One of the greatest disappointments I find in life, America, and the world is our lack of progress—the deterioration, in fact—in human relations. We have made notable progress in many technological areas—far beyond most people's imagination. That's great! At the same time, however, we find a deterioration in our family life, a challenge to the institution of marriage, a great disregard for the law and for the rights of our fellow man, a general moral decay, and a challenge to our churches as viable institutions. Someone recently said that we can put a man on the moon but can't figure out a way to get along with the man across the street.

Executive (50 to 59), insurance company, Virginia

My greatest disappointment with life today is that there are fewer and fewer people who are realists. Our society wants to do everything in theory, and this, I believe, is a big mistake. Many problems are blown out of proportion because no one is willing to sit down and evaluate them except in strictly theoretical terms.

Secretary and treasurer (50 to 59), manufacturer of hardware for electrical utilities, Illinois

My greatest disappointment is the ignorance on the part of the present generation with respect to our American heritage and the disregard for our democratic form of government which is the best in the world as we know it. I am also concerned with the internal abuses and disrespect for the flag and government as well as the loss of the meaning of the Golden Rule.

Director of utility services (50 to 59), North Carolina university

While the American idea of "manifest destiny" contained many problems, it nevertheless was the thought and dream that kept us bound together and gave purpose to our hopes and plans for a better tomorrow. Now, we no longer believe we have a destiny, and

much that was done from 1865 to the present is discredited, with nothing offered in its place. I see America adrift with no national purpose.

President (60 or over), life insurance conglomerate, California

My greatest disappointments have to do with the disappearance of "nature," with the difficulty in maintaining privacy, and with the difficulty in meeting and getting to know people without having to put up artificial façades.

Life insurance agent (30 to 39), California

The American way of life is a fabrication. There is no such thing. The concept has been coined by those in government as an apple pie and flag kind of argument. It is time we started thinking in terms of the "civilized way of life."

Director of engineering (50 to 59), metals producing company, Connecticut

I feel that a lack of responsibility to society in America and a deterioration of the work ethic have led to an absence of quality. One pragmatic example is the shoddiness of both goods and services in this country and the lack of interest among people to do any better.

Executive (40 to 49), electronics company, California

My greatest disappointment is business's disregard for the public interest. The real reason for inflation is the continuous price increases for products and services—and for no apparent reason. Business has taken advantage of a situation that could have been prevented. When controls were in effect on wages and prices, there should have been controls of profits as well. No one gives a damn for anything or anyone except themselves. Today's philosophy is "screw them."

Branch manager (50 to 59), savings and loan association, Illinois

My single greatest disappointment with the American way of life as it seems to be evolving is the loss of the Protestant work ethic.

President (50 to 59),
liberal arts college, Michigan

I am most disappointed with our seeming proclivity for war machines and war making. I have concluded that war is not instinctual, as many claim, even though aggression is a part of our personal human response to frustration and danger. I believe that if left to their own devices, people would prefer peaceful conditions. War arises primarily in response to the personal, political, and power strivings of national leaders and to the economic and professional motivations of munitions makers and professional war makers. The people, unfortunately, are relatively powerless unless roused by peace leaders, which doesn't seem to happen very often.

Another disappointment is with the narrow, selfish, shortsightedness of people—especially political, economic, and social leaders—in the developed parts of the world. But this is equally true in less developed parts of the world. We can expect the ordinary citizen to be limited in his perceptions and strivings because of limited perspective, but the problem is that leaders are limited, too—looking at things through their own "knotholes." This situation is reflected in the fouling of the environment, the wasting of resources, a throwaway consumerism, the push toward bigger and less efficient automobiles, moronic television "entertainment," and the slide into the "anything goes" philosophy of Watergate.

The only solution to these problems is intelligent, enlightened, and visionary leadership that can see beyond the immediate and gain the confidence of the people. But this is a tall order and it hasn't really happened much in our history.

Consultant to the United
Nations (50 to 59), New York

munism or Bolsheviks. I am concerned with the malady of Britian, Scandinavia, and Western Europe. As individuals and groups, we must fight the idea that Washington ("Big Brother") knows best. Wherever possible, we must return all power to local government units. Revenue sharing was the first step in the right direction. I am not convinced that the average guy wants big government as a father image. I am not positive that the bottom has dropped out. I remain confident in the American people.

*President (50 to 59),
consumer credit collection service
company, Indiana*

The drift toward socialism in the United States is frightening to me. Our citizens are being brainwashed by the liberals into believing that government can best solve all problems. People seem to be buying this philosophy more and more—and perhaps more so through passivity than through knowledge of what the government takeover of so many facets of our national life is doing to us. Somehow we need to stir up our people into understanding what the sacrifice of individual liberties will eventually mean.

*Vice president, sales
(60 or over), insurance
company, Minnesota*

There has been a creeping change in our way of life over the past 30 years or so with the acceptance of socialism and communism as another way of life. Generations are growing up completely ignorant of the basic concept of the federal-state relationship that has worked well. Many people now demand certain rights from the federal government which only increases the despotic power of the central system. The gradual, systematic destruction of the family as the basic unit of society through the takeover of parental responsibilities by the school system and the government—plus phony women's lib causes—will bring on the ultimate destruction of our free society. The

trend is irrevocable now. It will take a catastrophe of some sort to bring individuals and our leaders back to their senses, but the realization will only come while serving new masters in a slave state. I personally do my best to spread the word to my associates and neighbors. But few pay attention and few are interested in anything but the comics and sports pages.

*Project manager (40 to 49),
engineering and construction
company, Pennsylvania*

There is no question in my mind that the single greatest threat to our way of life is the fact that we see more and more socialism about us all the time. We see it in unions and local, state, and federal government. We read about it in newspapers, see it on television, and hear it on the radio. As our younger people grow up, it becomes part of their life style and there is nothing they can do to stop it. Although the majority of the people are against this system, there is nothing they can do about it because these are the people who are working for a living, day in and day out, and they haven't the time to carry signs in picket lines, to protest, riot, or check on their congressmen who are, more likely than not, not doing what they said they would do when they campaigned for office. To reverse this situation will take the kind of leadership in our country that spawns integrity, honesty, unity, and morality. Sadly enough, it appears that we have none of these people today—at least not in government.

*President (30 to 39),
manufacturing company, Ohio*

No the bottom is not falling out of the barrel, but well-intentioned people are refusing to become involved in the political process. Today, we are leaving politics to the politicians and that means that we will get even poorer results because politicians only seek power for themselves. This country will turn toward fiscal and moral re-

The American way of life is not what it used to be. Basically, all men were born equal—that is, entitled to the right to try to improve their lot. Today people believe they are entitled to the same things as everyone else by the mere fact that they were born. This is not the type of thinking that made this country great, and it will bring America to ruin.

Director of personnel
(40 to 49), Connecticut company

My greatest disappointment with the American way of life is the people. They have no respect for human life, property, or the feelings of their fellow man. For themselves, they have no integrity, lack the desire to accept responsibility, and take no pride in their work. Our country is deteriorating because of the prevalent attitude of "making it" at someone else's expense.

President (40 to 49), temporary
office services agency, Illinois

America has lost its purpose as a nation. We started out with the purpose of individual freedom to work for ourselves. We moved to subduing this continent and finally to providing enough goods for all. We accomplished all of this and now we do nothing. We have no sense of purpose—national or individual—other than self-indulgence. We need to establish national goals which again give individuals purpose. Perhaps the goal of providing enough goods for the world would be a start.

Treasurer (40 to 49), plastic
moldings manufacturing
company, Minnesota

The American way of life has become too commercial. We do not have enough love for one another. We really don't stop to smell the roses. We need to slow down and dare to be different—unity within diversity.

Personnel director (40 to 49),
hospital and college holding
corporation, Kansas

sponsibility when more bill-paying, hard-working, law-abiding citizens get involved in the election process.

*Executive (40 to 49),
chemical company, Michigan*

More people should raise their children in the "do without" atmosphere that most parents themselves were raised in. They should also teach their children more about respect for their fellow men. They should teach them to work for a dollar so they acquire a greater appreciation for it. They should teach them that "credit" is a privilege with obligations, and not a way of life. Finally, they should teach them that if love for God and country came before lust for power and fame, we'd be a much stronger nation. Our government leaders must realize that helping other countries should not be one of our endeavors until we have swept the cobwebs from beneath our own bed. Welfare should be denied anyone who is capable of picking up trash from our roads, parks, and forests. These United States have millions of fertile acres along our vast highway systems that could be planted with grain and sugar, providing work for the needy and at the same time reducing costs to the consumer. Unions should cease to have control of our government, and it should be put back into the hands of each individual American. When the unions scratch the backs of our legislators, then the legislators, in turn, must do some scratching. Our government cannot prosper in this kind of environment. Take the "fat cats"! If only honesty and pride could again dominate our lives, what a nation this would be! The sooner the American people realize that there is no way to get rich quick without hard, honest work, the sooner this nation will bloom and prosper again.

*Purchasing agent
(30 to 39), Texas bank*

A great threat to our way of life is the lackadaisicalness, permissiveness, and

indecisiveness of our judicial system—local to federal. We need to put some incentive back into being H.E.P. (Honest, Ethical, Patriotic). I am very concerned over our social and economic arrangements, and I am particularly concerned with what is happening in the political sector. After all, the political function largely controls the other two. I do not believe that the bottom will fall out of the barrel, but it could use some repair and preventive maintenance.

*General manager (40 to 49),
manufacturing company, Indiana*

The biggest threat to America is the laxity displayed by our judicial system. Specifically, crime *does* pay! This threat must be dealt with collectively by amending our Constitution or Bill of Rights to provide for a different way of dealing with the increasing crime rate in the United States today. My suggestion would be to change the "rules of evidence" to aid our law enforcement agencies and to provide for severe punishment for all crimes and misdemeanors. These changes must be reflected in the Constitution or the Bill of Rights in order to leave no leeway to individual judges.

*Tax director (40 to 49),
multinational/diversified
corporation, California*

The greatest danger to our society is permissiveness. Our governing bodies and courts must review and update laws to conform with existing conditions, and the courts must interpret the laws objectively. Habitual criminals belong in penal institutions where they should have to earn their keep. We should attempt to rehabilitate only nonprofessional criminals. Justice must be dispensed evenhandedly, not according to wealth or subjective thinking. Watergate justice is fine only if all the three-time losers in Washington are permanently put behind bars. Improvement in our laws and court system will give us the better moral climate we desperately need.

Vice president, manufacturing
(50 to 59), ceramic manufacturing
company, Pennsylvania

The greatest danger to the American way of life is the lack of discipline and regard for the law brought about by a liberal interpretation of the law by the judiciary. We are also witnessing the failure of leaders in government, labor, and industry and of parents in the home to set proper examples for the young and to teach them worthwhile moral and spiritual values. My concern causes me to support and become involved in organizations dedicated to preserving the American way of life. I am a member of my church council, the American Security Council, and the Institute for American Strategy.

Vice president (50 to 59),
manufacturing company, New York

Our biggest problem is the lack of protection of the people from the criminal elements in our society. We should begin to be less tolerant with repeated offenders. We should be a great deal more aware of our responsibilities in aiding our police and courts. We should stop protecting the criminal until we can guarantee victims the same protection.

Hospital administrator
(50 to 59), Hawaii

The American way of life is threatened by the rise in crime and the inability of politicians to work toward adequate solutions to this problem. Individually, we need to get involved in community police activities and to be more diligent in reporting crimes. Collectively, we need to demand changes in our jurisprudence system. I am very concerned that we are headed toward a confrontation with criminal elements that will not only injure our people, but will arrest our momentum as a country. Today, the barrel is floating on very rough waters.

Real estate sales and management
(40 to 49), California

I think that the greatest threat to the American way of life is the decline of moral values, which has led to an increase in crimes of every sort. To a great extent, this has been brought about by glamorizing the violation of law as "dissent" or "revolution." We are threatened by the downgrading of property rights and the encouragement of individuals to follow their own course without regard for others. Both individual and collective action will be required to change this trend—individual in the sense of more earnest parental efforts to instill the proper moral and ethical beliefs in children; collective in the sense of a reformed judicial system to permit swift and appropriate punishment for crimes.

Chairman (50 to 59), Texas bank

We are facing a total loss of faith in our government as a result of all the recent exposures of lies, cover-ups, cheating, plots, schemes, and the like of Watergate. It is hard to believe anything anymore when the president makes a statement. The so-called recession we are currently experiencing has not only disillusioned people but caused them to be just plain disgusted with the government for letting things get into such a mess. We have been asked to "WIN" when prices keep going up, more labor strikes are occurring, and unemployment is growing.

The American way of life has shifted in emphasis from an ethical way to a materialistic way. I am disappointed by the frantic search for material gain over spiritual and truly human welfare. We would rather, it seems, have a depression than allow inflation to trim our profits.

> Personnel director (40 to 49), fertilizer mining and manufacturing company, Idaho

Our country certainly has hit a low in confidence in its leaders, but we are not alone. Nowhere is there the strength and confidence needed to pull people together. It seems pathetic that only in times of national crisis (like World War II) do we really join in a common cause—and what a waste that cause, like most wars, turned out to be. The American Way has made everybody a Captain and we are drifting. We need a stronger hand on the tiller.

> Vice president, product support (40 to 49), construction equipment and materials company, Connecticut

"The American way of life" is contributing to the total world atmosphere of not caring. This country should lead the way toward the eradication of suffering. I am forever disappointed that "the American way of life" is all but blind to the way of life of the unfortunate and underresourced nations of the world.

> Vice president, administration (40 to 49), Maryland university

Today, we are too affluent, greedy, and individualistic—striving to perfect, improve, and acquire everything at any expense and with complete disregard for others. Strengthened by the Kennedy philosophy, a runaway Congress, and the Warren Court, people are led to believe that individual rights, expressions, or objections are paramount and protected under the guise of the law even though they are contrary to the will, desire, and want of the majority. While individual ob-

jectivity is declining—brought about by government example, actions, and directions—our entire democracy and legal fiber, which is predicated upon majority rule and common law, is subjugated to the will of the minority or the individual. We tend to no longer be a democracy, but an affluent, decadent society in a helter-skelter race to perfect ourselves and the world at any cost.

> Director of personnel and industrial relations (40 to 49), Virginia company

I think that my biggest disappointment is American business and the panic we see today as evidenced by short-term actions that will certainly fulfill the predictions of deep recession. In the final analysis, American business has no guts. What we see in the rest of the world is merely a reflection of what is occurring in our own country. The United States is the model and leader of the world. It has the strongest economy of any country and if we do not panic and take the action that our management training indicates, we can avoid the consequences of a crippling recession.

> Manager, market development (40 to 49), consumer products company, New York

There is a great lack of cooperation within the American community. How can we have world cooperation when there is no cooperation at home? Everyone is fighting for their rights—women, children, prisoners, Negroes, and gay people. There is no authority in the family. People are taught at home, at school, and at play that they should be independent—not that everyone should work together for the benefit of all: Tobacco will kill you, but the farmers and manufacturers will not stop producing cigarettes. Oil companies receive special tax benefits that other industries do not receive.

> Accountant (40 to 49), engineering company, New York

Money seems to be the name of the game, but if you don't have it you can't help small businesses or any kind of business for that matter. Hopefully, the powers that be won't get us into another war to boost the economy. I have a personal concern for the future well-being of our society because I have children who need to be educated and find jobs in the business world. Their college degrees seem useless because jobs are hard to find. I am also concerned about the economic situation, but do not feel that raising middle-income-level taxes is the answer—especially since upper income groups find all kinds of tax breaks and some actually pay little or no taxes at all. I am also concerned about our political arrangements. Can we change our luck by voting out all the incumbents and starting all over again? Also, how important is the vice presidency?

> *Marketing manager (40 to 49), manufacturing company, Pennsylvania*

Our greatest domestic threat is the decline in respect for the law and governmental institutions. This disrespect is the result of deterioration in religious values and the family unit. It is also the product of massive governmental inefficiency—including waste in the judicial and police systems. I am personally concerned about the future well-being of our way of life when most criminals go unpunished and economic crimes such as welfare fraud are conducted on a major scale while government officials wink at these crimes for fear of being called prejudiced against minorities.

Manager and financial analyst (30 to 39), manufacturing company, New York

In my opinion, the greatest single domestic threat to the American way of life today is the lack of trust in our leadership. Since the mid-1960s, beginning with mistrust of our political leadership during the Vietnam war and leading to lack of trust on the part of students in their educational leadership, this mistrust has spread so that today our business leaders, our religious leaders, our professional people such as doctors and lawyers, and almost every important element of society lack credibility with the general public. I believe this is making it ex-

tremely difficult for our various institutions to serve the public, since many people mistrust not only the ability of such leadership, but also the morality. I believe the public generally—and our leadership as well—recognizes that we must restore integrity and good character in all our dealings. I am hopeful that this realization will generate the necessary forces to restore credibility to our institutions and to our leadership. I believe that the United States has an excellent system of government, which, when exercised properly, will restore the confidence and regain the support of the people. There will be many unpleasant days ahead, however, before this can be achieved.

Banker (60 or over), Pennsylvania

The greatest single threat to the American way of life is the inability of our political institutions to modify and update their structures and processes to meet the needs of a twentieth-century world. The incredibly cumbersome Congress and the countless federal agencies compound the problems of today instead of being able to cope with them. Similarly, state and city

organizations are a mockery of even the simplest organizational principles. The ludicrous court systems are a monument of injustice perpetrated by vested legal interests and narrow legal minds. How to bring our system up to date is a mind-boggling undertaking that I must confess exceeds my talents. A few see these problems and must speak up as Chief Justice Burger has done. It is dismaying to note how little attention these problems have received from the academic, legal, business, and political intelligentsia from which reform must come.

Personnel director (50 to 59), chemical company, Missouri

We suffer from a lack of dedicated, competent leadership and management in most sectors of our society. Unless and until this changes, we will continue our ethical, moral, and spiritual decline. A change for the better will occur when the American people are willing to be led and to allow our leaders to lead.

Personnel manager (50 to 59), food processing manufacturing company, New York

A*mong the forces at work in our nation today that concern or alarm us are some that relate directly to our economic system and arrangements. Here, too, the influence of government is often—but not always—the target of criticism.*

The greatest domestic threat to our way of life is the subtle destruction of the free enterprise system and its free market mechanism. This system is being replaced by regulatory controls imposed by an ever-growing central authority—the government at all levels. The only way we can reverse this trend is to reduce the size of government and to reduce its role in the business community. It is frightening to me to note than in 1974 we passed a

highly questionable milestone. For the first time in the history of this country, government spending exceeded spending in the private sector. I am convinced that business will continue to be badgered and blamed for a growing list of problems which are not only affecting the nation's economy, but are interfering with the conveniences of the average American. These problems—like many before them—have been seized upon by a liberal-radical element in Congress and in the private sector and the academic community that would like to see the nationalization of American business. If this trend is not reversed, the bottom may indeed fall out of the barrel.

President (50 to 59),
flowers-by-wire
clearinghouse, California

The greatest threat confronting our country is the rush of thrusts to increasingly control private enterprise. This rush has been directed by bureaucrats and insensitive and utterly unaccountable meddlers. The rush is vocalized by a highly biased media. We face the bankruptcy of our healthy desire to excel, to build, to lead in constructive pursuits, and to function as citizens without a prostitution of career, mind, and soul. Control that stems from other than earned reward is damned and like its subject is doomed to ultimate spoil.

Executive (50 to 59),
electrical machinery manufacturing
company, Ohio

The greatest threat to the American way of life is the increasing intrusion of government into private enterprise. The American people will not be dictated to. They would not wear seatbelts on the order of the government. They will not buy 1975 autos because of the dictate on no-lead gasoline. Through influence and control, the government has caused inflation. Our free enterprise system is tough and demanding. It will work if the government will let it.

Data processing manager (50 to 59),
utility company, Michigan

While the American free enterprise system is not perfect, it has proven to be far better than any other method yet devised for providing citizens with an opportunity to obtain a good standard of living. We must do nothing to endanger the profit incentive under which that system operates. Without this incentive, the system will fail, and with its failure will go the benefits to

society that stem from the profits earned by corporations, both large and small, by small businessmen, and by the thousands of people who invest their savings in stocks, bonds, and savings banks, etc. From these profits come the money needed for the industrial expansion that must take place if jobs are to be provided for the thousands of new entries into the work force every year, if new homes are to be built, new churches, new schools, new recreational facilities, and the many other items that contribute to our high standard of living. In this regard, I believe that the greatest threats to our way of life lie in the degree of control being placed on the business community—including investors—by the federal government. Large corporations are attacked by liberals as being greedy and bad for society. But big monopolistic unions have virtually no controls placed on them and spend millions to elect the representatives of their choice who naturally lend their support to labor's socialistic viewpoint. All of this must be changed. The big unions should be subject to the same monopoly regulations as the corporations, and our laws should be revised to provide greater incentive to corporations and investors upon whom the country's ability to expand depends. Let's put the government controls nearer to home, and let's free up the controls placed on the business community. Let's permit it to operate in the true sense of a free enterprise system.

President (60 or over),
chemical company, New York

The greatest threat to the nation stems from a deterioration in the work ethic—productivity is down while wages are up and there is a lack of trust today between employers and employees. We need to embark on a national communications program to save our capitalistic system or we will continue to see more and more government interference in the running of business. When placing the most qual-

ified people into jobs becomes secondary because corporations don't want to wrangle with Uncle Sam in the courts, we can only look forward to the Gross National Product continuing to look bad.

Personnel director (50 to 59),
manufacturing company, Florida

The entire American industrial structure—our standard of living, our balance of trade, and our ability to withstand inflationary pressures—rests on maintaining levels of productivity which are superior to competing nations. The United States has yet to recognize this as a root cause of many of the problems experienced with the economy. Our entire system depends on efficient production in the industrial sector, and no amount of regulation of prices, wages, or interest rates will by itself solve these problems since none of these actions is of a generative nature. Japan has launched a concentrated program specifically targeted to outstrip the United States in industrial productivity by 1980 through the development and application of advanced automation techniques. A similar U.S. plan and program is urgently needed. The resources required and the cross-industry coordination essential to our success must be government-sponsored.

Director of international systems
(30 to 39), industrial process
control company, New York

Without question, the greatest single threat to the American way of life today is the energy situation. The shortage of energy in the future, should shortages continue, can be expected to change the life patterns and living standards of many Americans, and to shape the life patterns of the next generation. I believe that few realize today how serious the situation really is. A positive national program is needed to deal with this threat. Such a program was needed years ago, but is better late than never. The program must be aggressive and must be equipped with the authority to overcome any resistance. We must develop the means to provide energy for the comfort and transportation of our people, to supply industry so that good jobs and high employment rates can continue, to continue agricultural production at high levels, and to protect ourselves against those who would impose restrictions on our economic and political way of life. Negative approaches, such as resistance to atomic-powered electrical generating plants, fighting the development of coal production and offshore oil production, and passing laws against construction of refineries and power plants will impede progress to a dangerous point both for our economy and security. The positive program can protect the individual and the environment properly without force or direction from negative approaches to the problems at hand.

I do not feel the bottom has fallen out of the barrel, and do not think it will, but we had better make some progress soon toward solutions of our energy problems, or we can develop serious economic and social problems that could affect most of us.

Vice president, purchasing
(50 to 59), manufacturing
company, Colorado

The greatest threat to the American way of life is the decreasing productivity of American workers and the unwillingness of all workers (blue- and white-collar alike) to face up to the fact that wage increases should reward productivity increases, not productivity decreases.

Vice president, finance
(30 to 39), capital goods
manufacturing company, Maryland

I feel that the single biggest domestic threat to our country is inflation. At the present time our politicians will not face up to the issues. I believe that the main reason for this is that the politicians buy votes with giveaway programs. I believe that we are following in the footsteps of the Roman Empire.

My general feeling is that the situation is getting worse and worse and has reached the point where things are irreversible. I feel that our politicians are only interested in one thing—to get reelected. They will give the entire free enterprise system away just to get reelected, and we will follow in the footsteps of past civilizations.

President (60 or over), tool
manufacturing company, Michigan

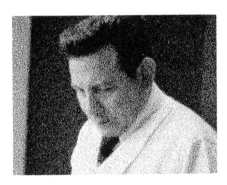

We are experiencing economic chaos. If we don't put our present economic system in order both domestically and overseas, there is a very real danger, in my mind, that our economic and political systems will not survive. I believe the danger is real and that our government and corporations are going to have to set aside their differences and work jointly toward a solution to our economic problems.

Distribution operations manager
(30 to 39), wall covering
manufacturing company, Ohio

I believe that inflation is the greatest threat to our national well-being. Inflation, I feel, is the result of 40 years of living beyond our means. If we don't begin soon to limit our national expenditures to our national income, our system will collapse in much the same way the German system collapsed in 1923. The German collapse resulted from a debt that was unmanageable.

Automobile dealer
(50 to 59), Maryland

The biggest factor threatening the American way of life is the lack of a basic understanding of fundamental economics. Industry must educate the

work force to understand the profit objective. From this base, industry can then achieve a more willing acceptance of the programs necessary to increase and sustain productivity. I find that people in the work force will perform well when they are told the facts in terms they can relate to. People need to understand the reason things are done the way they're done rather than just being ordered to perform in established ways.

General manager (50 to 59),
manufacturing company,
Massachusetts

In my view, the greatest threat to our way of life is our emphasis on institutional growth as fundamental to our socioeconomic health. Big government, having grown to unmanageable proportions, is the main culprit in this national disaster. Strategic planning at the highest levels is vital to getting us back on the right track. Planning must be done by the best pros in the country, and we must change our strategy and start moving in a new direction. We should lower our GNP expectations to 2 percent annually and emphasize not growth but an improvement in the quality of life. We should set optimum growth limits on virtually everything, and the government should set an example by reducing its size and the extent of its influence in our daily lives. I believe that I can best contribute by communicating my ideas and beliefs to my elected representatives.

Regional vice president
(40 to 49), contract food
services company, Pennsylvania

I think that the single greatest threat to the country today is monopoly. Monopolistic unions are causing a continual upheaval in labor costs without increases in productivity to offset these costs—the result is inflation. Monopolistic corporations such as oil and sugar grab off unreasonable profits and the result is inflation. Monopolistic government is "bought" by both through big campaign donations in exchange for special favors which strengthen the management/labor stranglehold over the American way of life. Also, under our progressive income tax system, inflation gives our monopolistic government a larger share of our earnings which continually reduces our real income. The only solution that I can see is to break up monopolistic unions and monopolistic corporations. Also we need to match wage increases to productivity gains. Otherwise, there will be no way to get our economy under control and to make the American way of life work for everyone.

Division controller (40 to 49),
Michigan conglomerate

The greatest threat to our way of life is the threat posed by irresponsible unions and the idea that every year everyone is entitled to a raise in salary whether or not employee performance (productivity) will allow companies to grant these raises without diminishing a reasonable return on venture capital and without raising prices. Another threat is the great disparity in wages to workers owing to the excessive economic power in the hands of unions—power given them by our government. What can be done? We need to establish guidelines through which salary increases can be eliminated unless productivity has increased as a result of either worker improvement or capital improvements. We should provide for a return of no less than the cost of capital to a company before wages are increased—even if productivity *has* increased.

Controller (50 to 59),
furniture company, Illinois

Unionization and the welfare system have been abused. At one time, unions were adequate and served their purpose well. Many people are now *too* protected and are working in positions that demand more than their abilities permit. There are also too many people on welfare who are capable of earning a living. This is the greatest threat to our nation today.

Bank officer (40 to 49), Indiana

*O*ther forces that we believe threaten our way of life today include a decline in self-confidence and individual initiative; a lack of pride in the work we perform and a decline in our standards of excellence; a growing tendency toward pessimism, cynicism, and despair; an increasingly permissive attitude toward mediocrity in much that we say and do; and a kind of national paralysis in the face of increasing social awareness and societal change.

The single greatest threat to the American way of life—and to all Americans—is the continued loss of our individuality. This trend began approximately 40 years ago and accelerated in the 1960s and 1970s. We continue to lean on, and expect the "other guy"—or the larger group—to take care of us. It doesn't really make any difference if that group is our employer, the union, the government, or whatever. We look to the group and not to ourselves to solve our problems. Pride, self-respect, and individuality are not clichés or textbook jargon. They are phrases which we once honored in this country. We can rekindle and regain these traits in our character. One man cannot do it and one organization cannot do it. We must start a campaign to collect many individuals and many organizations thinking alike to achieve this common objective. It will probably take another 40 years to return to individuality, but the future of our way of life, of America, is at stake.

Executive vice president and
general manager (40 to 49), data
communications products sales
and service company, New Jersey

more. Productivity in government!?! What an effect this could have on deficit spending. Individually, urban psychology combined with misdirected civil action has left us with a disinterest in "getting involved" never before seen on such a large scale in this country. A doctor fears to assist an accident victim without his expressed permission. An attacker is ignored by witnesses capable of stopping the attack. Collective security—a foundation of civilization—is seemingly neither collective nor secure in urban America.

Division manager (40 to 49),
utility company, Virginia

It seems to me that the greatest threat to our way of life is our diminishing confidence in ourselves, in our political and economic system, and in our leaders. The most dangerous of these threats is the loss of self-confidence—the weakening in our conviction that we can find solutions to our major problems and that we can willingly make the sacrifices those solutions may require. Similarly, our leaders lack the confidence to proceed with a program that requires a willingness to sacrifice or temporarily give up some of the comforts and pleasures our system has provided, but which cost more than we can for a time afford.

Executive vice president
(60 or over), insurance
company, Illinois

Americans are obsessed with material things. The American Dream is an advertising myth. Our educational system is obsolete and solidifies our prejudices.

Marketing consultant
(60 or over), Connecticut

Our rush to socialize or equalize all people kills the desire to grow ("Why work when I can be paid almost as much for not working?"). Next we will socialize our medicine so that we are all availed of equal treatment. This can go on and on to infinity and ultimate socialism. The answer is to edu-

cate people to realize that nothing is free and that each time we socialize something, we relinquish a freedom and this process does not reverse itself. I personally feel that this is one of our country's most serious and insoluble problems.

Operations manager (40 to 49),
manufacturing company, Washington

The greatest single threat to the American way of life is the loss of personal freedom and identity. We must try to reverse this trend toward more regimentation and the regulation of personal information that tends to reduce us to statistics. We must try to reduce our demands on the government to solve our social problems and ask more of ourselves in seeking solutions. We must drive our legislators to this end, individually and collectively. I am most concerned about the future well-being of our country. It's not too late to keep the bottom from falling out of the barrel, but it soon will be!

General manager (40 to 49),
manufacturing company, New York

The future well-being of our society would most definitely improve if our social, economic, and political arrangements were predicated on meaningful Christian values. A Christian way of life shows a healthy respect for all fellow men and women and nothing less!

Research and development
director (30 to 39),
meat processing company, Maine

It appears that too many young and old people today spend their time griping about their situation and looking for the easy way out. Specifically, too many people want something from the government or some other organization without having to work for it. This situation can only be changed by reinstilling a respect and joy for working toward a goal and relying on oneself and not on someone else.

Systems consultant
(40 to 49), Maryland

The domestic threat of greatest concern to me is the diminished sense of responsibility with regard to today's problems and our reaction to them. Politically, there is seemingly little interest in holding government organizations fully responsible for activities within their control or review. In response to the consumerism cry of the seventies, we are apparently headed for yet another federal agency. Few have seriously questioned the distinction between the "taxpayer" and the "consumer." Few have suggested that existing programs should deliver

We continue to face the growing grip of material requirements and have lost the rewards of inner peace and fellowship. Societal goals are directed toward a better "material" life—not toward a better place to live. This is not new and as long as we stay on this course our culture will continue to decay. We really only pay lip service to the needs of our fellow man. Corporations, in spite of the press for affirmative action and social responsibility, are still totally controlled by the profit motive. No one—no one is really willing to sacrifice.

Manager, market planning
(40 to 49), diversified
corporation, Minnesota

My single greatest disappointment today concerns the attitude of people in the United States. Far too many people downgrade the significant accomplishments of this country and ignore the fundamental characteristics that made our country what it is. They seem more interested in security than in personal or collective accomplishment. Too few are willing to take on responsibility to build for the future. So many are quick to criticize when they have no responsibility for, or stake in, the things they would change.

President (40 to 49),
manufacturing company, New Jersey

I am disappointed most by the lack of dedication, energy, honesty, and morality at all levels of government and to a lesser degree in industry and labor. The corruptibility of local governments, the judiciary, and the police is particularly enervating. The inability to cope with crime is frightening. The unwillingness of workers to give a full measure of production in return for their compensation is helping to make this country uncompetitive. Finally, the inability of managers to manage is adding to our ineffectiveness.

Certified public accountant
(40 to 49), New York

I believe that the American way of life is a wonderful way to live. But it could be better if the waste of funds and resources could be stopped and our efforts funneled into more productive areas.

Secretary and treasurer
(30 to 39), supermarket
chain, New Jersey

We are a people of too many biases—anti-Negro, anti-Vietnam veteran, etc. We need to develop a means for our people to gain a better understanding and appreciation of our traditional American "melting pot." America and its republic form of government can only succeed if we do away with the "anti-" complex that has permeated our way of life.

Executive officer (50 to 59),
federal government agency, Maryland

Too much importance is placed on financial success rather than on the value of the real character of the individual. The person who makes a great deal of money is, in most cases, automatically considered "smarter," a "leader," having "class." No matter what his or her personal character, a streetcleaner will always be looked down on, will never be accepted, and will be judged by the position he holds rather than by his individual virtue.

Executive (30 to 39),
New York corporation

The biggest threat to our society is the willingness on the part of more and more Americans to give up individual freedoms in exchange for collective security. This has resulted in a decrease in productivity and optimistic attitudes. We need to teach our children that discipline and productivity are the best tools we have for the retention of our way of life. We adults can help by providing a good example in our business and personal lives. The future gives me cause for worry. But I have faith that mankind will rise to the occasion and set new goals and overcome the challenges to our survival.

*President (40 to 49), lumber
manufacturing company, Washington*

The biggest threat to our total way of life is the lack of responsibility for the quality of life. We need greater integrity in work performance. We need to assume greater moral and ethical responsibility in the conduct of our business dealings. We need to accept greater responsibility in our communities with respect to housing, education, and human understanding. Our political and business leaders must demand integrity, quality performance, and sacrifice—worldwide.

*Customer service manager
(50 to 59), U.S. Postal
Service, Pennsylvania*

The greatest danger to the American way of life is apathy. We are running rampant with indolence, pessimism, cynicism, selfishness, and greed. Where is our patriotism? Where are the parents who love their children enough to discipline them? Where are the teachers who really teach rather than drift? Where are the school officials who are needed to support the efforts of our teachers? Where is the respect and appreciation for law enforcement officers? Where are the veterans who are not embarrassed to snap to attention and to throw Old Glory a salute as it passes by? Where are the preachers more interested in saving souls than in building the largest church in town? Where are the politicians who really mean and do what they say? What has happened to honor, pride, and duty? Where is our sense of humor? What has happened to our desire to excel? What has happened to individual courage? What has happened to basic honesty? I am worried sick over America's immediate future! We are into a moral vacuum caused by permissiveness and affluence. After things get worse and people get a gutful, then they will turn their faces to Heaven and start the long road back to rebuilding this greatest of all countries.

Insurance department manager
(50 to 59), farmers'
organization, Oklahoma

The greatest single threat to the American way of life is the willingness of people to let others make decisions for them. This is a form of apathy. The American way of life was built on a concept of individualism that developed strong leaders who were willing to stand up for principles. Little is done today in any field of endeavor that is not watered down before a final decision is made. Robert Lewis Stevenson wrote that "to know what you prefer, instead of humbly saying amen to what the world tells you you ought to prefer, is to have kept your soul alive." To this end, the soul of the American way of life appears dead at this time.

Vice president and controller
(40 to 49), financial services
corporation, South Carolina

Many people—particularly blue-collar workers, supervisory personnel, and middle management—feel that they cannot effectively influence the course of events. They have either forgotten or were never taught that man by his own efforts can change things. Part of the problem stems from the general climate of the enterprise—over-structured and stifling, for the most part. I am personally concerned about the future well-being of our

country to the extent that most of my consulting relationships are devoted to changing that thinking and to modifying behavior as much as possible. No, the bottom isn't falling out, but it's a long way up to the top.

Management consultant
(40 to 49), Michigan

We have a simultaneous decline in self-reliance and a rise in the "something for nothing" syndrome. As our population becomes less socially mobile and increasingly locked into classes, hostility spreads between the "haves" and the "have-nots," with each trying to get as much of the pie as possible, preferably by doing little or nothing for it. Some of our legislators are doing their best to make this process respectable.

Senior vice president
(40 to 49), Ohio company

The greatest threat to the American way of life is the lack of opportunity in this country to starve to death if one is so inclined.

Lobbyist (40 to 49), Idaho

There is an increasing tendency at the political level to suppress the individual, his aspirations, and his creativeness. Within unions and large corporations, the individual has become lost under the weight of "mass action." This is a vital and critical mistake that is being perpetuated throughout our society. There is little room left for individuality, and if this trend is not reversed, it will destroy our ability to further strengthen the American way of life and to bring the greatest good to *all* of the people. The bottom is not falling out of the barrel, but it has developed some ominous cracks.

Manager (50 to 59),
chemical company, New York

The greatest threat to our way of life is the rise in the socialistic attitude that the government is able and is obligated to provide and to care for all citizens. People should serve the government instead of government serving the

people. We must return to an attitude that each person must provide for himself and that those who will not work will not be supported by those who do. My concern is that unless we stabilize our government and return it to a sound fiscal and social base, both our government and the capitalistic system will fall. I do not intend to lose my country, my form of government, my business, my way of life, and the free enterprise system without pledging all my abilities and resources to preserving it.

Owner (50 to 59),
construction company, Oregon

The average worker no longer takes pride in performance. Everyone now asks, "What's in it for me?" or takes the position, "I will do as little as possible just to get by and even less if I can get away with it."

Business manager (40 to 49),
school district, Pennsylvania

My greatest disappointment is the accelerating demise of "rule by law" and personal freedom. I believe the basic failure involves our "one man, one vote" concept of democracy which encourages our elected legislators to buy the votes of vocal, special interest minority groups at the expense of the silent, divided, and increasingly ineffective majority. The immorality and inequity of this process are destroying our national morality and concentrating control of our destiny in the hands of an incompetent bureaucracy.

President (50 to 59),
specialty chemical
manufacturing company, Minnesota

The single greatest disappointment I find with the American way of life is the emphasis on "things" rather than ideas.

Consulting civil engineer
(30 to 39), Massachusetts

The American male is being relegated to a self-concept of a "team member" as opposed to a member of the team who should not delegate his right of individual opinion, energies, and accountability. Unfortunately, many of us have learned too well the art of delegation. We now have a society of career survivalists instead of individualists.

President (30 to 39),
educational consulting and
child care firm, Georgia

In the United States today there is an enlarging gap between "have" and "have-not" Americans. This causes too much injustice in law, education, and health.

Data processing manager
(30 to 39), Maryland university

My big disappointment is the emphasis voiced by upper-level management on volume and quantity instead of on quality. They demand quick profits rather than long-lived business relationships. I am also concerned about our failure to allocate sufficient capitalization to ensure success in new ventures. I am concerned about the frightening inability of people at all levels to communicate verbally. Finally, I am concerned about the incompetence of the majority of people in mid- to upper-level management.

Product repair administrator
(30 to 39), transportation
equipment company, Maryland

I am distressed that within America we no longer look forward confidently to a greater, richer, happier tomorrow. We can salvage our remaining resources—good air, clean water, and unspoiled space—only by sacrificing some degree of economic growth.

Senior vice president, finance
(50 to 59), insurance
company, Michigan

Despite a higher standard of living, better educational opportunities, improved health care, housing, and mass communications, the rate of crime in the United States has increased to the point where a whole way of life that used to exist in our cities is disappearing. This is a great loss of our freedom—the freedom from fear.

Vice president, manufacturing
(40 to 49), manufacturing
company, Ohio

My main concern is with the increasing pressure for conformity. By insisting that the rights of all groups be protected (and this is a worthy objective—one I fully support), we are enacting laws which promote a "play it safe" mentality. We have created undue penalties (legal, social, and economic) for those who dare to be different or innovative—or who do not follow the "normal" rules.

Senior executive (40 to 49),
transportation company, Ohio

I am most disappointed by the "indifferent" attitude that people display today. They are not willing to get involved and create change, and are too willing to accept things as they are.

Personnel director (30 to 39),
sporting goods manufacturing
company, Iowa

We have assumed a posture in this country that overlooks the need to evaluate "contribution" as a measure of one's worth to society. In its place we have, through false and misleading notions, assumed that society is to be evaluated on the basis of that which it contributes to the individual without the need for the individual to contribute in return. No society that claims that equality is to be measured in terms of financial status—equal housing, equal medical treatment, etc.—can attain greatness. Unless we can redirect our political system to once again focus on providing individuals the opportunity and the right to achieve according to a combination of ability and effort, we will attain only the mediocrity that some people call the "classless society" and that pulls all greatness down to the level of the "faceless average."

Personnel director (30 to 39),
publishing company, Missouri

I believe that the United States is about to undergo a serious threat to its future, centering on the lower financial class's growing awareness of the destructive morals and values of an increasingly selfish, corporation-dominated, lying upper class. The political factions in our society are showing themselves by their actions to be clearly caught up in the morals and values degradation—that is, they are acting in the interests of the profit-sick ideology of the power corporations and other special interests.

Drug abuse counselor
(under 30), Florida

There is a definite threat to the American way of life. That threat can be stated in one word, and that word is "greed." In recent years, greed has been one of the dominant forces in our society—politically, economically, and socially. This has become evident in the Watergate incident which needs no explanation here. What primarily concerns me is the overzealous greed in our economic system. Our system is

based on an ever-upward spiral of more and more. As the spiral continues, more and more wealth is concentrated in the hands of a few, and people become polarized between the "haves" and the "have-nots." The obvious results are strife, tension, and unsettled conditions. Another obvious fact is that the spiral cannot continue. We live in a finite world with limited resources, while our system is based on the opposite point of view. This has led to the rape of the environment and a plastic-paved world of alienated people. There is little or no respect for the land, the world of nature, and people in general. They are all treated as "things" to be used, manipulated for the sake of the "bottom line."

It seems to me that we must work toward a more benevolent type of capitalism, or, to use another term, an industrial democracy where *all* people share in the fruits of their labor, not just the few. Profit cannot be the only motivation. I am not advocating eliminating profit, but I am saying that we should be interested in more than profit. We need enlightened leaders—executives, presidents, foremen, etc., who are interested in people. It may sound utopian, but we need people who can get along with less materialism, less "things," less profit, less Gross National Product, so that we can get to the basics of living, and enjoy life as it is meant to be enjoyed.

People must be recognized for, and share in, the work they do. This is a basic human need which is being ignored in our system today. If our present methods continue, I can only have a very somber, negative outlook on the future. Also, this recognition must go beyond people. We must develop a "land ethic" which treats our natural and wildlife resources as part of us, not as separate "things" only to be used and exploited.

In some respects, yes, the bottom is falling out of the barrel. As stated above, our present directions, if continued, can only lead to eventual catastrophe, but there are segments of our

society, especially among the younger generations, which add a ray of hope to the future. There is a "back to the basics" movement, a care and concern for people, our world, and *all* the parts of it. There *are* segments of our society which are less concerned with materialism and exploitation and which are achieving "the good life."

After all, isn't our purpose to be in a loving relationship to one another and to enjoy the beauty of the world around us? We are far afield from this way of life, but there are positive forces in our society which are calling us to these goals, whether they be in the social, political, business, or religious areas. I, for one, want to be in that camp.

Regional sales manager (40 to 49),
office supply company, Minnesota

The American way of life is based on a concept of individualism that is essentially opposed to collective well-being. This is the real danger in the years ahead. Our political and economic leaders, for the most part, are motivated by self-satisfying objectives. Our free enterprise system is affected by the same self-satisfying objectives, reflected in the ever-increasing hunger for more profits, to the detriment of the social responsibilities that most corporations have to be forced to accept. I am concerned for the future well-being of our society, and believe that we should concentrate in our educational system on building our youngsters' minds toward their collective social responsibilities rather than stressing individual success in terms of our present materialistic standards and concept of life.

Executive (40 to 49),
hotel chain, Washington

The greatest domestic threat to America is the growing attitude that "whatever is right for me is right" or "since I have only one life to live, I should do whatever I feel I want to do." In my opinion, no society can survive for an extended period of time if people are not concerned for one another and don't work to leave this world a better place for future generations. The bottom of the barrel is not falling out, but it is weakening. I see the younger generation starting to take the opposite approach in that younger people seem now to live for the future and for future generations. I believe that the only real solution is to find a leader. John F. Kennedy was a leader and Nixon could have been one if he hadn't lost contact with the real American people. The American public, in my opinion, is desperately looking for leadership.

General manager (30 to 39), agri-cooperative, Iowa

The greatest threat to the American way of life is the growing conviction that every person is entitled to a high standard of living regardless of the contribution he or she makes to the national wealth. This belief excuses individuals from making personal efforts to contribute and results in frustration when people don't receive what has been promised. I believe this is why more and more people are attacking the system, including the government, employers, and institutions such as our churches and schools. This condition has also led to a breakdown of the family, which is becoming merely a social rather than a social *and* economic unit. I believe that people will come back to a more logical view of life and their respective rolls in it after facing the painful consequences of political and economic readjustments. I am personally concerned and preach my confidence in the human race and its future whenever possible.

President (40 to 49), commercial finance company, Connecticut

Individual Americans have lost the will to resist temptation in many areas of our national life. We forgo moral principles in pursuit of immediate personal gain. Most of us have delegated the right to prevent crime to the "other guy." We don't want to be involved.

We shy away from participating in investigations of what's happening in our governmental processes. We are failing to tell the "business story" to our children. Finally, academia has not been educated in American moral traditions.

Controller (50 to 59), textile company, South Carolina

Individually and collectively we are asking for a larger share of what is in the barrel and show very little concern for assuring that enough goes into it to satisfy our needs and demands. The bottom won't fall out, but there will be nothing left for any of us unless we assume responsibility for seeing to it that we provide the bounty we require. Big Brother won't make it happen. Indeed, by playing politics, Big Brother is speeding the wasting of our labors to satisfy selfish interests.

President (50 to 59), manufacturing company, Massachusetts

The greatest threat to the American way of life is cynicism and despair. I believe that the three major foundations of our society—the schools, churches, and the home—have been attacked by unexpected and overwhelming forces of change. Their basic understanding of themselves and their roles in a fast-moving and rapidly changing society does not permit them to change fast enough to withstand this attack, and they are in danger of failure. I am committed to continue working toward the strengthening of school, church, and home. We have a leaky barrel, but the bottom will not fall out.

Chemical engineer (50 to 59), Texas company

The greatest threat to the American way of life is an overdependence on our political processes to perpetuate our way of life. There is a definite lack of initiative and self-confidence being exhibited by the generation that will guide the next 50 years. There are too many people in—or about to be as-

signed to—positions of leadership who are looking and waiting for political answers to economic problems. Our social system and culture were not developed by the government (although its influence was considerable), but by the people. In our homes, schools, and churches, we need to return to helping young people to understand what made this the greatest country on earth. We need to help them to understand that our pioneering families did not wait for unemployment compensation checks to arrive before doing positive things. They did not listen to labor union bosses while making commitments to their employers. I am concerned, but I am confident that our young people are smarter than my generation was and that they will return to or develop a system of values different from the one we see at the present time.

Vice president (30 to 39), Nebraska bank

The greatest single threat to the American way of life is the weakening or erosion of the family unit through creeping moral decay. We can best deal with this problem through strong personal family relationships and involvement in business, church, political, and community activities that exemplify high standards and ideals. I do feel that unless our business, religious, and political leaders become more responsible, the bottom will fall out of the barrel. Maybe it will take this kind of a shock to bring our nation to solidarity.

Treasurer (40 to 49), wholesale distribution company, Utah

The political changes toward big government and socialism, the punitive laws directed at business, and the monopoly of unions are the greatest dangers facing America. The liberal press, owned by a few liberal groups, dominates the average citizen's awareness. With repetition, any lie becomes true, and the average American believes the lies the liberal press puts out and he votes accordingly. The American Dream of "rags to riches" is dead or has been taxed to oblivion to support a few minorities and striking workers.

Research manager (40 to 49), research and development organization, Pennsylvania

Families are no longer as close as they used to be. Children see parents in a light that has left them in a state of bewilderment. It is no wonder young people have lost respect for their elders. We have forgotten to teach our children right from wrong.

President (50 to 59), metal reclamation company, Ohio

Radical college professors are alienating the leaders of the next generation. A great number of our most promising young people are leaving college with an antibusiness bias. Business must insist that its side of the story be represented in the faculty. Businessmen must go out to our colleges—perhaps as adjunct professors—to counter the radical doctrines. College administrators must be persuaded to present a balanced view of business—not just the radical one.

Manager (50 to 59), chemical company, Virginia

The greatest threat to our country is the unwillingness of the powers that be to honestly face up to the problems of change and social awareness both within the United States and abroad. We need to organize change rather than try to keep it in check.

Financial manager (30 to 39), food industry, New York

Individuals are unable to express their concerns without becoming a part of a "group" or pseudo-minority. I also believe that too many Americans are poorly fed and educated. My present concerns are limited, as our institutions, while undergoing change, do seem to have the ability to adapt and to meet their responsibilities. The contrary is true with respect to the notion

We have lost our enthusiasm for life. It appears to me that many Americans have a very fatalistic outlook. It's almost as if we are looking forward to failure or want to experience hardship. We have lost some of our self-confidence and are feeling sorry for ourselves rather than rising to history's most awesome challenges. Add to this the idea that we as a nation are in a political rut and suffer from a severe case of lack of leadership.

Manufacturing manager (30 to 39), cosmetics company, New York

We have failed to teach minorities—especially blacks—the value of personal pride and work. Being "minorities," one would expect a special awareness on their part which seems to be lacking and should be taught. Our biggest fault is in rewarding a substandard performance on their part which if done by a white person would be punished in some way. This attitude is a form of discrimination. No one in this world gets something for nothing—or do they? Bigot?

Operations specialist (30 to 39), Illinois bank

The American way of life is still the best. However, my greatest disappointment with it relates to greed and power. Politics no longer consists of representatives for the people—this has become a secondary instead of primary priority. The American people are being misled more each year, and really who can say just how far this will go before we put a stop to this cancerous growth through rebellion or something similar?

Manager, data processing center (30 to 39), Alabama company

I am disappointed by the fierce fighting for material gain at the price of ethics—public officials who betray public trust, businessmen who are unethical, ripoff repairmen, and dishonest employees.

Executive vice president, corporate affairs (50 to 59), engineering company, California that the bottom may be falling out of the barrel: I believe that by June 1975 our economy should have turned around and the food problems of a number of underdeveloped countries should begin to look up. By January 1976 the general world view should be good.

Consultant (40 to 49), Texas

In simplistic terms, the American way of life is best summed up by the belief that if one is honest and works hard one will achieve success, happiness, and wealth. To me, this is a cruel myth which, having been discovered to be just that by members of minority groups and others, has led to disillusionment, frustration, and apathy. This reaction has led to violence, crime, and drug abuse, and to a frighteningly low turnout of registered voters at election time. From the middle of the seventeenth century until roughly the end of World War I, America was a land of opportunity for those who embraced the Puritan work ethic. Many factors, including our vast natural and land resources, an influx of cheap foreign labor, low taxes, unlimited energy, inventive genius, and huge markets within our own borders, plus a freedom of movement and freedom from so much government control, offered unlimited opportunity to those willing to work hard for their dreams. Although great opportunities still exist, restrictions on achieving them are harsh and the Horatio Alger theme of "any boy can become president" is tempered by the conditions of political reality and the necessity for millions in campaign funds. I believe that we now find ourselves at a point that marks the end of one era and the beginning of another. We must bend with the winds of change—and if we Americans insist on preserving that form of government and a society that is the envy of the world, we can do it! We can do it if we are willing to recognize the aspirations of people as individuals and not as numbers on a production line. We can do it if we recognize that our educational system is not accountable for the product it produces and are determined to do something about it. We can do it if we are willing to use self-control rather than governmental controls; if enough of us are willing to enter politics to help our communities, states, and nation; if we are interested enough in electing leaders rather than followers to public office even though we may not always agree with them; if we will take the time to study the issues before we vote; and if we are sincere enough to practice our religion enough to judge a person by his or her character rather than color. My answer to your question concerning the greatest threat to the American way of life is "the average American citizen."

Board chairperson (60 or over), hydraulic equipment distributing company, South Carolina

The biggest threat today to the American way of life is "the American way of life." The whole concept of a nonreturnable, nonrecyclable, plastic society is not viable. The ideals incorporated in a way of life that hails "a new car every two years," everything packaged in plastic and cellophane, and the dumping of industrial wastes into the air and water cannot endure on a finite planet with a growing population. Ten or 20 years ago was the time to chart a new course to correct the consumptive abuses that are now so prevalent in our society. Nothing was done then, little is being done now, and no long-range plans for the future have been drawn up. With no planning, things tend to be done in the worst possible way. I see the end of the American way of life in the immediate future. This wouldn't be so bad, but because of a lack of preparation, I also see much suffering ahead for our people as changes in the quality of life are forced on them by events.

Self-employed businessman (under 30), Missouri

The greatest threat to the American way of life is our permissive attitude toward mediocrity. Over a long time span, the essence of the American way of life has been to reward outstanding performance and the exercise of unusual talent. While it is entirely appropriate to help people to enter all walks of life in our society, we cannot do so at the expense of lowering our standards or rewarding as satisfactory personal performance that is clearly inferior. Further, we have the affirmative duty to encourage in every possible way those who use their talents effectively. In this sense, personal attainment, entrepreneurship, innovation, and the profitability of our institutions must be promoted and recognized as the mainspring of our way of life. I am concerned about our future well-being. But there is still time for effective corrective action—particularly with respect to governmental activities—if we act promptly.

Assistant to the president
(50 to 59), diversified
corporation, Connecticut

The greatest threat to the American way of life is the deterioration in our standards of excellence and in the disciplines necessary to sustain them. We are becoming a nation of ''average'' guys and gals—in what we think, say, and do. We are threatened by the loss of our ''leading edge.''

Vice president, planning
(60 or over), consumer products
company, New York

I fear the power of the press and television to propagandize in the name of reporting the news, and thereby to mold and influence the thinking of literally millions of people. I fear the unimpeded use and distribution of data from ''a reliable source.'' I fear the violation of the individual's right to privacy and the destruction of his personal and professional reputation—sometimes undeservedly so—in the name of the public's ''right to know,'' in contradiction to our legal heritage

which specifies that a person is innocent until proven guilty. I abhor the apparent absence of a sense of fair play and equal justice in the dissemination of news, and the production of one-sided, biased, and frequently inaccurate television documentaries and specials which are sometimes more emotional than factual. I fear the attitude of omnipotence frequently demonstrated by the media in their ''right'' to be the sole judge of what the public sees and hears, regardless of whether or not the information was legally obtained, adequately verified, detrimental to our national security, destructive to our foreign policy, damaging to the reputation of the individual, or encouraging to the mentally ill to commit sensational crimes which, coincidentally, become themselves further items of ''news.''

Director of management
engineering (40 to 49),
hospital group, Texas

I believe that the biggest threat to our way of life is the failure of the media (radio, television, and the press) to fulfill their obligations to society. Completely free from malpractice liability and consumer protection liability, the media today seem more inclined to control the direction of events and to draw their own conclusions for the reader, listener, or viewer instead of presenting unbiased, factual, and balanced reporting of events. Society as we have known it cannot endure with a government run on the basis of popularity polls. With the leisure time of Americans at an all-time high, it is sad to see the quality of the media at an all-time low. The only hope for improvement lies with the next generation.

Restaurateur (40 to 49),
chain operation, Alabama

The news media—both electronic and printed—are, in my opinion, the greatest threat to the American way of life today. The national networks should be removed from the air, and

I am very disappointed by the revelations surrounding Watergate. I have lost faith with all in high political office and am concerned about who truly represents me. Our young people see our apparent double standards and question our real motives. I agree with them.

District manager (30 to 39),
communications services
company, Indiana

What is the American way of life? This expression has a different meaning for each individual. Moreover, whatever yesterday's meaning, today's is different. To me, in my youth, it meant opportunity, freedom, and prosperity for the individual who had the necessary ability and who was willing to work long and hard to accomplish objectives. Ability and effort controlled one's degree of success. Today, the American way seems to be dedicated to forced success (through artificial or legislated measures) though confiscation of personal resources and liberties to provide equal benefit to all without regard for individual qualifications or effort. I do not disagree with equal opportunity for all, but challenge an American way of life which could destroy that which made this country great.

Executive (60 or over), life
insurance company, Pennsylvania

I am most disappointed by the unwillingness of a majority of individuals to take action to correct wrongs or injustices and to achieve the objectives they wish—with the consequent effect that vociferous minorities attain objectives that are not always the will of the silent majority.

Corporate treasurer (50 to 59),
real estate company, New York

The most disappointing state of affairs today is the probability that there is no turnaround for America. America used to mean something—something different to each person, but still something over which we had control. Man can

no longer control his destiny. He works in jobs that do not satisfy. He is told that he doesn't have to stay where he is, but—logically and realistically—he is muchly trapped by his circumstances. Too many people have lost everything or too many believe that they are the masters of their fate and captains of their destiny. Where, oh, where is reality and practicality?

Personnel manager (40 to 49),
life insurance company, Texas

People are not honest with one another. They say one thing and do another. This can be found in all walks of life—in business, in government, and in community life.

Systems manager (30 to 39),
health care organization, Illinois

My greatest disappointment is to have worked hard to reach an economic level at which I thought I would be comfortable, only to find that inflation and taxes have reduced my purchasing power to a point which makes it a struggle to get by. I find it increasingly difficult to believe in the "work ethic."

Operations officer (30 to 39),
New Jersey bank

According to the media, unless you're "in" you're "out"—out of the real mainstream. And who are the "ins"? The high middle class to wealthy. The mature young (a contradiction?). The

fair-skinned and blue-eyed. Those people who affect other people's lives in an obvious way (the famous, big shots, bosses, attorneys) to the exclusion of the "common" man.

Manager of personnel development
(40 to 49), city government,
New Jersey

The demise of our free enterprise system is my single greatest disappointment with the American way of life. Chief Justice John Marshall warned as early as 1819 that "the power to tax involves the power to destroy." He might have added, moreover, that the road to destruction is the road to socialism. It began with the Federal Income Tax Law of 1913 which gave unlimited access to the people's wealth and the power (for the first time) to levy taxes not only for revenue but for social progress.

Excessive taxation produces results somewhat resembling the evils of slavery and serfdom in days of old. Lenin, that implacable foe of the free enterprise system, predicted as early as 1920 that the United States would eventually spend itself into bankruptcy. He also added that "taxation with its offspring, inflation, is the vital weapon to displace the system of free enterprise." Let's have lower taxes and put a limit on governmental power—and just maybe we'll survive another 200 years.

Systems analyst (40 to 49),
New York bank

each local station should do its own news programming. I realize that the chances for this are indeed slim because the networks excuse their wrongdoing by screaming "Freedom of the press!" Someone once said that freedom of the press belongs to those who own it. I do not think the bottom is falling out of the barrel, but the networks are sure trying to make that happen by their biased reporting. All the news is bad—nothing good—in the social, economic, and political areas.

*Purchasing director (40 to 49),
transportation equipment
company, Georgia*

The greatest threat to our way of life is our indecision with respect to utilizing the means at hand to solve internal technological problems. We don't utilize the means at our disposal because they are not palatable. Unless we begin to move in this direction, however, the exponential nature of our problems will exclude solution without revolutionary dislocations.

*Chemical engineer
(40 to 49), manufacturing
company, Pennsylvania*

My gravest concern has to do with the public indifference to overpopulation and the dangers inherent in continued population growth. People don't seem to realize that overpopulation is not something that has happened to us. Overpopulation is something we have done to ourselves.

*President (40 to 49), diversified
corporation, Delaware*

The greatest threat to the American way of life results, in my opinion, from worldwide overpopulation. The resources of food, fuel, minerals, and clothing production are simply not adequate to meet the increasing demands resulting from the population growth. Unless educational procedures and medical assistance are forthcoming soon, the American way of life will deteriorate rapidly.

*Treasurer (50 to 59), aircraft
manufacturing company, Kansas*

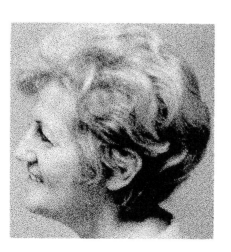

The twentieth century has been called "the American century," and our country's influence on human affairs, in peacetime and in war, has clearly been monumental. The many contributions to international development and human well-being made by American education, science, and technology are all but indisputable. But the current century has also been one of wars and rumors of wars, of death and destruction, unparalleled, many claim, in the world's long history. The same inventive genius that has sent a few men to the moon has also sent millions to the grave, and we haven't yet learned how to really live peacefully together.

We want to say a few words here concerning what disappoints us most about the world that we live in. There may be little that is new in what we have to say, but what is important here is the number of old problems that remain unsolved— problems of aggression, ignorance, and hunger, problems of intolerance, misunderstanding, and greed. Old habits die hard.

We also want to talk about the twentieth century. Has this century—on balance—been chiefly a period of progress for mankind or one marking the decline of civilization and sensibility? It is difficult to assess 75 years of staggering change in a few words. But while most of us agree that this century, to date, has been a mixed bag of progress and problems, we are hopeful about the future and confident in our hopes.

2

THE WORLD AND THE 20TH CENTURY

On balance, I would say that the twentieth century has been, to date, chiefly a period of progress rather than decline. There are, however, a number of significant problems yet to be resolved in this century. On the positive side, we can see a general worldwide increase in the standard of living, a reduction in worldwide death rates, improved control of major diseases, increased worldwide food production; increased awareness of the need for protection of the environment, and a greater interest in fostering the "rights of man" throughout the world. Some of the dangers and challenges include: Can the various nations of the world achieve a reasonable level of cooperation, recognizing their interdependence in economic, political, and social situations? Will mankind be able to prevent further misuses of technology? In the past, these misuses have resulted in environmental destruction, wars, and world starvation. If technology is properly utilized—and priorities for sensible action developed—the real needs of mankind can be addressed. The problems of food production, population control, health, and housing can be reduced if the nations can agree on these priorities and work together.

Executive (50 to 59),
environmental protection
systems company, Illinois

The twentieth century has been a period of progress in terms of per capita GNP, industrial and agricultural production, etc. More important, the problems concomitant with this material progress—maldistribution of income, poverty, cyclical fluctuations, social maladjustments—have been recognized as such, and methods of solving them have been developed and are being applied.

Investment banker
(40 to 49), New York

I believe that the twentieth century has passed the "peak" of civilization and sensibility and that we are today in a

period of permanent decline. I believe that the key factors that have led to this state of affairs are overpopulation, overconsumption, and the realization that continuation of present patterns will soon lead to intolerable pollution, depletion of resources, and even more inequitable distribution of wealth and greater disparity in living standards. There are simply too many grave continuing crises—the Arab-Israeli conflict, famine, Vietnam, northern Ireland, oil and energy shortages (economic and political maneuvering), etc.—which convince me that mankind is becoming increasingly desperate and irrational. I believe a major cataclysm will occur by the year 2000.

Corporate planner (40 to 49),
metallurgical products
company, Massachusetts

As yet, the twentieth century is neither a century of progress nor decline. It is a period in which prior structures and modes of civilization are being shaken apart by tremendous forces of technology, population growth, and mass communication. Out of this shaking apart, a whole new culture may emerge or civilization may collapse into another Dark Ages. The critical issues facing us all today are population growth and worldwide resource allocation.

Director of computer systems
development (30 to 39),
U.S. government
agency, Maryland

The twentieth century has been chiefly a time of progress. Technology has helped us a great deal in coping with increasing population. It has provided for increased food sources, a better living standard for many, better means to control the resulting pollution, and new means to provide for future energy needs. Social conditions have improved. There is greater racial tolerance, more effort to seek peace, and the need to control population growth has been recognized as well as the necessity to aid the world's unfortunate. Business and government are working better together to solve all kinds of problems. The pendulum is swinging in a positive direction, on balance.

Corporate marketing director (40 to 49), industrial products company, Illinois

If we examine the twentieth century in the aggregate, it has been a period of progress. We have had wars, economic problems, social problems, and the like. However, we have come through these with better and stronger resolve with respect to the future. The technological advances have been great—space travel and spinoffs. These breakthroughs will keep us moving onward, in my opinion, in many fields of human endeavor. The computer, television, and nuclear energy are tools for social and economic progress that we haven't nearly exhausted. Much forward thrust will result from our recognition of human rights and the generation of new technologies arising from today's beginnings.

Purchasing agent (50 to 59), refractories producing corporation, Pennsylvania

In the areas of technology, personal wealth, and education measurable advances have been made. Arguments that technology is progressing toward its own grave don't hold up. In any society the most obvious alternative to work mechanization is slavery, and we don't want that. Today's environmentalists are even contributing to technology through their efforts to force new air and water pollution control equipment. In spite of recessions, inflation, and dollar devaluation, the average American still has increased his actual net worth during the twentieth century. Also, more individuals obtaining more years of formal education constitutes real progress. A civilization begins to die when it tends to exist only for itself to the exclusion of its environment. While the United

States has become a bit more nationalistic recently, the members of the world at large have become more involved with each other's problems, thanks to progress in communications. Sensibility tends to remain constant over long periods. The basic morals of our people and their personal goals and aspirations have not changed significantly during the twentieth century in spite of what the media might say to the contrary to sell its wares.

Marketing manager (40 to 49), multinational corporation, Pennsylvania

The twentieth century has been primarily a period of progress. The advance of science has been tremendous and has been very heavily influenced by advances in communications. There are virtually no "country rubes" left in the United States, and they are disappearing in other countries as well, largely because of better communications. "Future shock" is creating a lot of problems, but I feel things will work out for the better in the long run. I don't consider myself a starry-eyed optimist, but I think there's a lot of hope for man and his world.

Office manager (30 to 39), New Jersey company

I believe that the twentieth century is characterized most by the rapidity with which changes have occurred. The turbulence of change has had an impact which is little understood. At the least, it gives each generation a taste of all the world's kaleidoscopic

panorama of possible events—recessions, booms, social and political upheavals, wars, scientific achievement, and all the rest. This is experience of the most fundamental nature, and through experience the human race adapts and survives. (It could destroy itself, but one must believe that it won't.) This revolutionary process has got to be good—a kind of progress, if you will. It's certainly an exciting, wonderful time to be alive. I wouldn't want to miss it for anything. We may be living through the adolescence of mankind, so to speak.

Vice president for technology (40 to 49), chemical company, New Jersey

The twentieth century has brought its share of disappointments, but the evidence of progress marks it as a century of advancement for mankind. Individuality has never known such progress. The growth of information—reflecting scientific advancement and recognition of philosophical/technical interrelationship—is many multiples of the growth of knowledge in previous centuries.

Executive vice president (50 to 59), manufacturer's representative, Illinois

To date, the twentieth century has been preoccupied with the advancement of technology. This has produced a "thing-oriented" society. However, cycles come and go, and there appears to be a trend toward a reemphasis on people. Scientific management has been replaced by humane management—management that focuses on *doing things with people* rather than *through* them. Vietnam kindled a concern for life rather than for "victories." Consumer advocates and other people-oriented groups have been established. People are insisting on being treated as individuals rather than as computerized numbers. If these trends continue, society will be the better for them.

County librarian (40 to 49), California

DISAPPOINTMENTS WITH THE WORLD

The single greatest disappointment I see with the world today is in the inability or unwillingness of world leaders to offer the world a system of moral, ethical, and concerned leadership. I believe that world resources are adequate for the world, but too much is controlled by too few. If our world leaders were ethically, morally, and humanely concerned about the total world population, many economic/resource inequities would probably disappear.

Vice president (40 to 49),
Maryland university

My greatest disappointment with the world is our inability to translate Christianity into national goals of the United States and other countries. I am also disappointed with substandard education that leads to population growth beyond the world's ability to adequately feed the majority of its people.

Chief executive officer
(50 to 59), Illinois company

I have just returned from a trip through the developing countries. My greatest disappointment with the world is that the governments of these countries are doing far too little to rapidly develop ways and means of feeding their starving people. Resources are being wasted on far less important things such as atomic armaments, etc. A total effort must be made to improve food production and to industrialize in order to provide more jobs for the poor. Also, the developed nations should be providing more unselfish assistance to aid in feeding the starving people of all countries.

Professor (60 or over),
Michigan university

The twentieth century will be looked back on as one of the most radical periods of change in history. A review of the many major accomplishments in technology will be recognized as the foundation for advancements in the future. Even with 8 percent unemployment, we still can be proud that 92 percent of our people are gainfully employed—and this is due to the basic quality of our people.

*Director of management systems
(40 to 49), higher education
institution, Illinois*

There is no doubt, in my opinion, that the twentieth century has been chiefly a period of progress. All one has to do is to look around and see the evidence of mankind's great achievements: man has walked on the moon, solved vast problems with computers, made giant medical advances, and increased his standard of living. Along with these advancements in technology have come advancements in the areas of racial and sexual equality, with a greater focus on "rights" in general. I feel that many people are "down" on the twentieth century as a result of these advances in technology and human freedom. They view these advances as vices which threaten to consume us and spell the decline of our civilization. For example, many people question new-found freedoms and ideas in the areas of marriage, family, drugs, and pornography as agents to destroy our civilization. Technology has also created changes such as possible loss of pride in work, faster life styles, and living with the threat of total destruction. These are all real problems; however, I feel that these are not sufficient to mark the twentieth century as the "decline of civilization."

In conclusion, I restate my belief that the twentieth century has been and is one of tremendous progress in all areas. True, we have our problems; however, when we see the whole picture (from Kitty Hawk to the moon in 70 years, conquering of diseases such as polio, the right to vote and work

regardless of race or sex), there is no doubt that the twentieth century is a century of incomparable progress.

*Materials manager (under 30),
manufacturing company, Virginia*

Without question, the twentieth century has been one of great progress in virtually all areas—technology, medicine, transportation, communications, living standards, education, social reform, and many others. Of course, it is always the case when people are involved that progress will also incur some mistakes, "bad apples," and other negative aspects. But in no way do these negative factors combine to tip the scales toward an overall decline of civilization and sensibility. In spite of our present-day problems—that I believe to be temporary—I am enthusiastic about the future.

*Personnel officer (40 to 49),
insurance company, New York*

The twentieth century has been a period of progress, not one of a decline in civilization and sensibility. Technology has advanced rapidly and proven the "prophets of doom" wrong. Today one farm worker can produce enough food to sustain 45 people, whereas in 1820 the average farm could only produce enough for four people. We, in the 30 to 40 age group, know the technology that has resulted in the airplane, radio, television, and space travel—a technology that is sometimes taken for granted by Americans. The "prophets of doom" have for years predicted overpopulation and lack of food for the world, but due to mankind's initiative and technology these have not come to pass. Fifty years ago plastics were nonexistent and today there are many applications of plastics where once steel or wool was used. The use of plastics also extends our wood resources. In summary, we are a greater nation, capable of meeting today's problems and challenges because of our ability to utilize science and technology.

Manager (30 to 39), manufacturing company, Tennessee

I feel that the twentieth century—on balance—has been chiefly a period of progress rather than one marking the decline of civilization and sensibility. It has recently become fashionable for people to yearn for the return of "the good old days." But they are only half right: the good old days were certainly old, but they weren't really all that good. To paraphrase a popular women's lib slogan, "We've come a long way, baby!" A person born at the turn of the century, if fortunate enough to survive the epidemics of childhood diseases, had a life expectancy of about 50 years. Men reached their educational peak early—at the age of 18—after completing high school, and could then look forward to working 50 to 60 hours per week for the rest of their lives. Working conditions were often unhealthy, and work itself, often routine and monotonous. Women worked nearly all the time on household and family chores. People often lived their entire lives without traveling more than 100 miles from their place of birth. People had little, if any, time or opportunity for cultural, charitable, community, or even recreational activities. Minority groups were restricted in their educational, employment, and housing opportunities. Women, in addition to these restrictions, were not even allowed to vote. Many people lived below the poverty level—ill-fed, ill-housed, ill-clothed. Many people suffered from physical and mental ailments because of inadequate health care facilities.

Today all of these conditions have changed for the better. Our life expectancy has increased to 70 years—the Biblical three-score and ten. Through preventive vaccines, we have eliminated the threat of smallpox, typhus, scarlet fever, whooping cough, and polio. Through community schools, night schools, and correspondence courses, continuing education opportunities are available for everyone, regardless of age or income. The average work week has decreased to 35 to 40 hours. People now have more time to spend with their families and to improve the quality of their lives. Improved working conditions have made work more pleasant. Job enrichment has made work more meaningful. Household appliances have freed women from much of the drudgery of household chores. Improved transportation facilities have permitted people to travel more and to enjoy the beauty of our country. Our philosophy of "providing a hand, not a hand-out" has enabled families to rise above the poverty level. Our spirit of concern and fair play has gone a long way toward providing minority and lower income groups with equal voting, educational, employment, housing, and health care opportunities. How did all of these improvements come about? These improvements have occurred because our country is made up of people who care—people who care about themselves and who care about other people.

Senior vice president, marketing (50 to 59), health products manufacturing company, Pennsylvania

My global concerns focus on the fact that most of the people of the world live and will die hungry—and there is no improvement in sight. There is no program on the horizon that can relieve "want" in the poorer countries.

Senior vice president (50 to 59), insurance company, Michigan

My greatest concern about the world today is the vast population explosion. This situation is very much like uncontrolled cell growth in the human body—cancer!

President (50 to 59), mobile home industry, Georgia

As a young man I began to experience a gnawing concern about what the fate of the world might be if its population continued to grow. Modern science was giving us "death control"—but what, I wondered, about "birth control"? More than 30 years later, what do we have? Vast areas of the world face starvation. Pollution of land, air, and water is rampant. Welfarism is sapping our economic resources to feed spawning millions. My greatest disappointment with the world as I find it today is the fact that my generation has made so little progress in achieving worldwide understanding of this most basic problem—uncontrolled population growth.

Personnel officer (50 to 59), New Jersey bank

My single greatest disappointment with the world today is the apparent lack of progress in retarding the population explosion. The population growth momentum seems bound to aggravate international tensions, to deteriorate the quality of life generally, and to accelerate the depletion of our

finite supply of raw materials. It is thwarting both internal and external efforts to improve the physical well-being of people in many poor countries. It will put increasing economic pressure on the more advanced countries which have achieved some degree of population stability.

President (60 or over),
newspaper advertising sales
company, Connecticut

My greatest disappointment with the world today is our inability or unwillingness to stop population growth and its resultant corollaries.

Head of systems division
(50 to 59), New York company

I am most disappointed by the enormous amount of the earth's resources ($240 billion annually) that are dedicated to military purposes.

Data processing manager
(30 to 39), New Jersey university

I am most disappointed by the fact that men and nations are still aggressive and adversary toward one another.

Research and analysis
(30 to 39), Police
Department, New York

I am most disappointed by the continued use of force by nations in achieving their goals and by the limited ability of the United Nations in mediating these conflicts between nations—the Mideast situation, for example.

Executive (40 to 49),
Kansas utility

Mankind is unwilling to profit from its history and experience. We have learned 10,000 times over 10,000 years that warfare is not only wrong, but also unnecessary. Yet we continue to dissipate our resources on the never-ending building of armaments.

Director of engineering
(50 to 59), metal
producing company, Connecticut

In my opinion, the twentieth century has been one of magnificent progress on the part of mankind. Not only has there been tremendous technical progress, allowing man more and more freedom from the drudgery of eking out an existence, but there has also been a very substantial—if sometimes explosive—amount of progress in social fields. Technological progress is readily apparent, and also manifests itself in many areas of social progress. The movement of mankind toward a one-world feeling of social responsibility has been very significant during this century. Although some of these movements have required cataclysmic lessons—such as the two world wars—the move has been very real and conscious. More individuals are truly free today than ever before, and this is the result of the technical and economic creations of the twentieth century.

Numerous problems remain to be solved, but the mere fact that they are recognized today as problems and that attempts are being made to solve them indicates the tremendous progress that has been made in man's social consciousness and awareness in this century. Most of today's problems are the result of having solved a past problem. For example, overpopulation is primarily the result of having solved past problems of disease, famine, and pestilence. The problem of a shortage of energy is primarily the result of the burgeoning demand for energy, and the fact that many, many more people are in a position to make these demands.

All the progress mankind has made in the twentieth century is merely a foundation for more progress to be made in the twenty-first century. Man's outlook today is substantially better for the world, for nations, and for individuals than it has ever been.

*Vice president, finance
(40 to 49), manufacturing
company, New York*

Technologically there is no doubt about the progress made during the twentieth century. The advances have been greater during the last 25 years than during all of history before that. With technological improvement there has come a slight improvement in sensibility and civilization. Although conditions exist in the world that seem outrageous to the average American (and seem therefore to indicate a decline in civilization), most of these situations have existed for centuries and have only come to light because of modern technology.

*Personnel and finance manager
(under 30), manufacturing
company, Indiana*

The twentieth century reflects an era in which man's native wit is confronted by diminishing marginal returns when perceived through past aspiration levels. It has been, however, an era of tremendous scientific growth and exponentially increasing social demands. The genius of man will be tested by his ability to comprehend and solve these difficulties amid ever-escalating resource costs, population demands—and within a democratic framework.

*Research analyst (30 to 39),
U.S. government, Virginia*

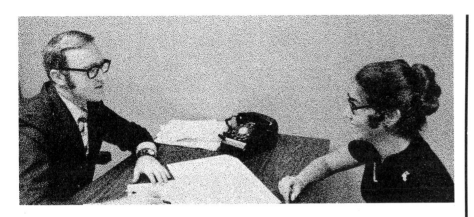

Never before in the history of mankind has the opportunity for economic, social, and cultural equality existed as it now exists in this country. Technological advances have made life more comfortable than ever before. We've paid a price for this progress—in diminishing resources, pollution, etc.—a price which some believe has been too great. We cannot, however, return to the eighteenth- or nineteenth-century style of living and still provide the economic, social, and cultural advantages available today. Increased research and further technological advance (coupled with a greater awareness of and regard for our environment and the quality of life) will solve those problems which seem beyond solution today.

Vice president, systems
(40 to 49), insurance
company, Illinois

I feel that the twentieth century has been one of such enormous and rapid progress that it has outstripped our ability to adjust to it psychologically. This inability to adjust has led to some confusion as to whether or not we are really making progress—and to some reaction against further progress. I believe that the enormous pace of progress was made possible by the great advance made before World War II in our understanding of chemistry at the molecular level—and since, as a result of the development of computers. The contribution made by computers rests not so much on the adding of new knowledge, as on enhancing the practical utilization of mathematical concepts which have been accumulating for centuries, and which were too complex for practical use before the development of the computer.

Executive (50 to 59), chemical
company, Tennessee

The twentieth century has certainly been a period of rapid advancement. To qualify this change as good or bad depends on one's frame of reference. For one who has difficulty in adjusting to rapid change, the differences in mores and ethics are difficult to accept. This type of person might view the present state of civilization as being in a period of decline. I, however, feel that the state of the world today is much more honest and realistic than in former times. A larger segment of our population is aware of the choices available on any issue and is more aware of the freedom the individual has to make a choice. With less flak from others about the choices you make, there is a more accepting atmosphere than formerly. I would tend to think that civilization is in better shape today than ever before.

Nursing administrator (30 to 39),
New York hospital

The technology of this century has led to such communications and mobility advancements that I believe it marks the beginning of the family of man and the end of factionalism. Granted there is much ignorance, prejudice, and blind rationalism, but nothing like there was during the entire previous history of man. There are just too many people today who see and feel humanity and themselves as common

The great emphasis on militarism, coupled with the ignorance of leaders who in many cases are brought into positions of political power through violence, bodes no good for the advancement and the well-being of the human race.

Assistant treasurer
(60 or over),
Tennessee organization

The greatest disappointment I have with the world today can be broken into two areas. The first is the waste of our natural resources and our total lack of concern in this area until recently. The second is that so much money is being spent on armaments and other ridiculous things rather than spending the money on improving the quality of life for the millions of people in the world who are starving.

Secretary and treasurer
(30 to 39), supermarket
chain, New Jersey

Many of the world's governments, including our own, find it necessary to allocate disproportionate amounts of money to defense expenditures. Some leaders who have suggested a more rational approach to defense spending are ridiculed by business, labor, and the press. Yet, these expenditures contribute virtually nothing to our standard of living or our feeling of well-being. It might even be argued that our feeling of insecurity increases as defense spending consumes a greater part of our national income.

I would also brand as a myth the popular belief that high defense spending is necessary because it provides jobs. Surely, our national leaders are capable of developing a peacetime reconversion program which could utilize the skills and facilities available to solve our most pressing national and international problems. I see little hope for a meaningful solution to our problems until we come to grips with the problem of the military-industrial complex and our "role" as the world's policeman.

Executive (40 to 49),
transportation company, Colorado

passengers on spaceship earth for the barriers and isolationism born of man's previous limited visibility to continue to exist. It may take three to five more generations for this new concept to dominate the policies and practices of individuals, organizations, and nations, but I believe it will. I believe it began in the twentieth century, and I believe it is the most important progress that mankind has made to date.

Quality control director (30 to 39), integrated circuit manufacturing company, Florida

The twentieth century—and I have lived through more than half of it—seems to me to be most notable for its scientific advances. The changes in moral values and standards that have developed along with the achievements in science are really no more remarkable than similar drastic departures from traditional mores in past centuries. I believe that people today are even more sensitive and sensible in their relations with one another and the environment than were their forebears. This is due in part to the development of the ''world neighborhood'' through increased travel and better communications.

General counsel and secretary (50 to 59), insurance company, New Jersey

Prior to the twentieth century, life was at best difficult for all but the very wealthy. Homes were poorly lit, poorly heated in winter, poorly ventilated in summer. Sanitation was crude. Animal wastes and raw garbage polluted the cities and farms to a horrendous degree. Men spent most of their lives in physically hard labor, starting at tender ages, working long hours with little if any respite for their entire lives. Woman's lot was as bad or worse. Many farm families wore out two or three homemakers. For the masses, individual rights were nonexistent. Communications and transportation prior to this century limited influence spheres to tiny localities. The territorial imperative was pronounced. Superstition substituted for culture and knowledge. The twentieth century's technological developments in industry, agronomy, and the sciences have freed mankind from much of the crippling effort prior ages required simply to stay alive. This freedom in conjunction with the startling progress made in transportation and communications is projecting civilization into the idealistic dream of the ages—a one-world, family of man society.

President (40 to 49), manufacturing company, Wisconsin

M*any of us have generally positive views about the twentieth century, as you have seen. Some of us, however, believe there is much to be done on the social and intellectual fronts despite remarkable advances in the sciences and technology.*

The twentieth century has been a period of almost unimaginable progress in a technical and material sense. Methods and approaches for transportation, medicine, and communications—to mention only a few—have surpassed earlier predictions. However, progress with respect to basic human thinking, understanding of one's own nature, and the ability to understand and describe mankind's fundamental utility and purpose is not much changed for the better at all. One need only to read the writings of previous inhabitants of the earth, such as the authors of the great books of the Western world, to see that we have contributed little in our time to human understanding. Perhaps the Industrial Revolution with all its marvelous contraptions was a necessary step in freeing mankind from drudgery so that future generations can devote their time to better understanding and appreciating that beautiful and mysterious entity we call "mankind."

Head of research and engineering (40 to 49), hardware manufacturing company, California

To talk about progress in civilization and sensibility is to talk about the parallel development of technology, culture, and the awareness of individuality. The twentieth century has telescoped progress at such a rapid rate that change is often indiscernible. But a backward and forward glance offers evidence that progress has indeed been made. At the beginning of the twentieth century in the United States, technology was in an embryonic state. Our century has since offered us television, transistors, pocket calculators, computers, air travel, moon walks, and interplanetary exploration.

Such a tremendous rate of technological growth has generated new cultural growth: the intellectual and aesthetic faculties of the people of our century have changed dramatically. For example, the knowledge explosion caused by rapid technological growth has made a "Renaissance man" an impracticality. Instead, our century has produced the "specialist," usually grouped in teams to provide support systems for continuing technological growth. New electronic capabilities and synthetic materials have also lent to the artist a greater freedom for expression. Witness electronic music, steel and plastic sculpture, and the use of film as a new art medium. The emergence of the knowledge specialist and of greater artistic diversity has resulted from technological growth and both of these emergences have

signaled an increased interest in the individual. Gradually, the twentieth century has seen a new awareness of the rights and plights of the individual, resulting in the various rights movements—"one man, one vote," affirmative action programs in industry, a war on poverty, and above all—as a result of Vietnam—a growing awareness that war is not glorious, that no one wins. If such an awareness can remain in those who possess it, and if it can spread to others, this will mark the greatest historical contribution of the twentieth century toward mankind's progress. It will ensure that mankind will have a continuing history, one marked, hopefully, by a respect for life.

Training manager (under 30), insurance company, New Jersey

We could view the twentieth century as one of progress if progress were measured in terms of technological advance alone. But it is both obvious and disappointing that the evolution in man's ability to intelligently use that which his imagination has contrived has fallen short. Although man has gone from using horsepower in the early twentieth century to nuclear power before mid-century, he has not likewise progressed from "horse sense" to "new sense." In point of fact, the situation seems to have regressed with respect to man's ability to cope with the physical, emotional, and behavioral ramifications of technological progress.

Manager of EDP operations (30 to 39), New York bank

I would say that the twentieth century has been a period of great progress as far as technology and medicine are concerned. I believe that socially there is yet a lot to be accomplished, since the advance of science has been much faster than the human adjustments to it. I personally admire the American way of life and the latitude and opportunity there are here for a person to grow in his or her professional field if one tries hard enough. I also believe there is still a sense of justice in this country. By the way, I am a *woman* professional engineer.

Structural engineer (30 to 39), architectural/planning company, Florida

The twentieth century has been the most progressive century to date as far as technological advance is concerned. The accompanying social ills may make it appear to be a period of decline for the American culture. The remaining 25 years of this century offer a tremendous challenge to all people—especially for Americans. In *Management: Tasks, Responsibilities, Practices,* Peter Drucker explains how today's institutions must fill a void which their formation created: the need for individual self-fulfillment, environmental protection, and improving the quality of life in general.

General manager (30 to 39), safety equipment distribution company, Texas

I believe that the twentieth century most definitely has been a period of progress in terms of technical advance, health care, and industrial growth. Unfortunately, progress in these areas has not produced a more complete and happy civilization. Man has been racing in circles, seeking happiness and peace. We need to better channel our energy in the direction of helping one another achieve this end.

Staff accountant (30 to 39), engineering and architectural company, Missouri

The twentieth century is marked by great progress—but in a structured sort of way. Plus marks must be given to research, science, and technology. But only the term "mediocrity" can be used to characterize organizational development. Human advances have not kept pace with technological ones. Thus, the man-machine system is out of balance. The increasing gap between the rate of technological progress and the human condition poses a

challenge to the management of resources. Since change is upon us, we need to take a thorough look at the impact of technology on people. The problem of progress is a technical, human, and organizational one. Its solution should be approached through examination of all three elements, which are interrelated and must work together. The pacing factor may be the lagging one—people.

Management consultant, information technology (50 to 59), Virginia

The twentieth century has been a mix of progress and regression. On the one hand, we have been able to land men on the moon less than 75 years after man first learned to fly. Yet reactions to events based on primitive emotions have led to almost continuous warfare. Great strides have been made in all the sciences, yet starvation is rampant throughout the world. In this country, education has been raised to its highest level but only as a result of Supreme Court decisions and the use of federal troops. There is no question that the twentieth century has been a period of fantastic progress, but people are still primitive in their interrelationships. The twenty-first century must witness the harnessing of all the technological and scientific skills available to correct the shortcoming of human emotions.

Sales manager (under 30), telecommunications company, New Jersey

The twentieth century has been and continues to be a "period of paradox." On the one hand, man's progress, technologically, has been excellent; on the other, man has regressed, emotionally and spiritually. Through the years, man has always been and will always be either the beneficiary or the victim of his leadership. If my conclusions are correct, man has experienced growth in his technological leadership and a decline in his moral, ethical, and spiritual leadership. The two are probably related in the sense that as mankind develops technologically, he pays more attention to the material side of life and less to the nonmaterial aspects.

Personnel director (40 to 49), chemical company, Pennsylvania

I believe that the twentieth century has been a period of much progress in terms of technological advance and in releasing people from various forms of bondage. Looking to the future, it seems that greater emphasis must be placed on developing the worth and responsibility of the individual.

General manager (50 to 59), power supply company, Minnesota

The rate at which man's knowledge has grown during the twentieth century has to mark it as an era of great progress. Mechanical inventions have lightened man's workload, resulting in more free time. We have experienced the benefits of scientific advance-

ments, new medical methods, better transportation, and a new awareness of other human needs. Any decline in civilization and sensibility is primarily due to man's ill use of his new free time and his attempts to indulge himself personally, the "liberal" attitude toward the court system, and the breakdown of family life.

Owner (40 to 49), steel service center, Ohio

The twentieth century has been a century of progress mostly. Much of this progress can be attributed to technological improvement. However, I have observed no particularly significant change in mankind or human nature. Thus some of the horrors of the century (as well as the progress) are due to the unvarying nature of man, who now has much greater power for both good and evil.

Professor (30 to 39), California university

My single greatest disappointment with the world is the lack of knowledge of right and wrong (and selfishness) on the part of young people. They are the products of what my generation has made them. They are faced with real problems because to them whatever they do is right because that is what they want to do. No longer can school materials be shared. They disappear, so that only one student can read and study them whenever he or she likes. There is a constant struggle for top grades, and anything one student can do to another to keep him from making the grade is just part of the game.

Professor (50 to 59), Alabama university

I am most disappointed by mankind's continued inhumanity to mankind in spite of historical repetition and the greatest technological progress the world has ever known.

Safety director (30 to 39), aerospace company, California

My greatest disappointment with the world today is the need for dishonesty.

National sales manager, consumer products (30 to 39), chemical company, New Jersey

Nations continue to forget the lessons of history. Power is no guarantee for continued viability. Greed, pride, and propaganda have killed more people than heart disease.

Director of corporate planning (30 to 39), plastics manufacturing company, California

My greatest disappointment with the world today is the greed of nations and their inability to settle differences— even by force.

Program administrator (40 to 49), support services organization, New York

We have not learned from history how to live together without war, greed, and continually seeking power.

Manager (40 to 49), manufacturing company, Pennsylvania

The world's inhabitants are unable to live together peaceably. Even our international peace arm, the United Nations, doesn't seem sincere in its efforts to resolve differences between nations. Peace is not a high enough priority item for most countries. Each has its own selfish interests which come first.

Plant manager (40 to 49),
chemical company, California

Social and political institutions throughout the world have failed to act constructively toward enhancing communications and solving recognized worldwide problems.

Business manager (40 to 49),
aerospace research and
development company, California

Much of the world's attention, energy, and resources are still being expended on wars, revolutions, dictatorships, and terrorist activities. After all the tragic lessons of history, this has to be the greatest disappointment with the world today.

Vice president, manufacturing
(40 to 49), Ohio company

I am most disappointed by the inability of the people of the world to live in harmony, following the Judaic-Christian ethic of brotherly love.

Officer (30 to 39),
California bank

My greatest disappointment is simply the lack of cooperation between nations.

Accountant (40 to 49),
engineering company, New York

The world has yet to learn that it is one and that what harms one will somehow harm all. The crises created by certain groups or interests for their own personal gain will eventually turn on them if they continue to do their things at the expense of others.

Manager of personnel development
(40 to 49), city
government, New Jersey

My greatest disappointment with the world today is the apparent lack of understanding that human beings have about life and its purpose. More specifically, it is the failure to realize that we are one world and that the value and purpose of living has been best evaluated by those principles Jesus expressed in the Sermon on the Mount 2,000 years ago. Most human beings are encapsuled in their own universe, of which they comprise the center, and conduct themselves accordingly. Greed and self-interest destroy those values conducive to true culture, and the continuance of life on this planet is in question because of this. It is discouraging to see this emphasis upon materialism at the expense of more enduring values. True empathy, charity,

and brotherly love are not entirely lost arts, but they are not very popular. Those individuals in control of the economic and material resources on this planet have the power to end, or vastly reduce, not only the quality of living, but life itself. Many of us hope that they will become more aware of their responsibility.

Management consultant
(30 to 39), Minnesota

There are so many conflicts between nations and people. There seems to be more hate and distrust than love and trust.

Title not indicated (30 to 39),
Kentucky company

The single greatest disappointment I find with the world today is the unwillingness or inability of nations to work together to solve very critical world problems like population growth, resource depletion, pollution, and food production and distribution.

Civil engineer and consultant
(30 to 39), Massachusetts

My single greatest disappointment with the world and with the American way of life is mankind's singular goal for the gain of material things. The reasons for inflation, and the recession that has followed, lie in the fact that everyone wants to gain material wealth above that of his neighbor. The results are people who can be

"bought" or people who will compromise moral standards to achieve their material goals. We see this situation running rampant in our law enforcement agencies, our schools, our government, and the clergy. This condition was very aptly described by the prophet Micah when speaking of the children of Israel. The end result for them was defeat and destruction. It may well be the same for us.

Field director (30 to 39), religious organization, Alaska

I am most disappointed by the selfish, materialistic view of life assumed by most people.

Personnel director (40 to 49), mining and manufacturing company, Idaho

Despite the fantastic advancements in human knowledge and technology over the past few years, the world, for the most part, seems bent on following the same basic trends that have characterized the general history of mankind. It seems that man, individually and collectively, is dedicated to the principle of serving only his own interests, with little regard for the effect of his actions on others. There seems to be little, if any, realization that driving one's fellows into ruin and destruction can only lead to ultimate chaos and disaster for everyone.

The universal needs for food, energy, and monetary stability are becoming more disproportionate day by day. It seems to me that the whole world must come to the realization that there is no sacred store of value which can possibly withstand the onslaught of a world in complete disequilibrium. Certainly a way will never be found to equally distribute the world's riches, but it seems to me that we should be working on the problem of finding what the breaking point is and what adjustments must be made before that point is reached.

Senior vice president (30 to 39), large commercial bank, Pennsylvania

Most people do not live up to their own potential in terms of mental and spiritual abilities. Too many refuse to "grow" in the concept of helping their fellow men.

Director of personnel (40 to 49), Kansas hospital

My greatest single disappointment with the world has to do with the selfishness and greed of people and nations as evidenced by their inability to solve international problems through cooperative action and discussion. The near (impending?) failure of the United Nations illustrates the point.

Manager (40 to 49), electronics firm, California

The greatest disappointment with the world today as I see it is the lack of unity achieved among countries. With the knowledge we have gained about our world during the last 50 years, we have done very little in working toward a world economy. Nations are by and large still nationalistic. Some have given millions away trying to ease their consciences and believing they are working toward a world economy. But their actions have only brought contempt.

Director of personnel (40 to 49), insurance company, Connecticut

My greatest disappointment is over the way people treat each other. Our behavior leads to crime and international conflict. Too many people put material gain ahead of everything else.

Research and development manager (50 to 59), large industrial company, Illinois

The world has not learned the true meaning of "peaceful coexistence." There is still a lack of trust between all countries, and the inability of the large powers to agree on almost anything restricts any successful conclusion to the near state of war between many small countries.

Chief executive officer (50 to 59), manufacturing company, New Jersey

In *The Organization Man,* William Whyte, Jr., observes that "people grow restive with a mythology that is too distant from the way things actually are." Most of us agree that a wide disparity exists in America today between the "social fiction" (the cultural mythology, the promise of the American Dream) and the "social fact" (the realities of human experience). Many of us believe this disparity is growing, while others do not feel this way. Some of us believe it is a stimulus to further individual or collective achievement, while others view it as a crime or as a shortcoming, at least, in our efforts to extend to everyone the benefits of the more abundant life.

All individuals are subject to certain delusions—and whole cultures too! And we believe that America is no exception. In this chapter we also want to talk about some of the cultural delusions many Americans are under today. What are the origins of these delusions and what can be done to clear away the misimpressions they foster in the public mind?

To begin with, we examine the "social fiction" and its relationship to "social fact" in our society today.

SOCIAL FICTION AND SOCIAL FACT

Our founding fathers placed great stress on the freedom and opportunity extended to all. This remains the "dream" and the "fiction" of the American way of life. Race relations and economic deprivation are still big problems. Employment stability has not been realized. Educational opportunities vary greatly from state to state, within cities themselves, and between cities and their suburbs. We alone among civilized nations do not have a system making medical health care available to all. Religious intolerance is a fact of life in banks, insurance companies, and elsewhere in industry. Now, in the depths of a depression, the glaring inequalities in our society stand out in bold relief and the American Dream remains a dream for many.

President (60 or over), industrial technology company, Michigan

The disparity between the social fiction and the social fact is a wide one in American society. The social, economic, and political complexities of our society present a depressingly overwhelming barrier to anyone attempting to achieve the American Dream. Business is no fun—accomplishment consists mainly of living through crises. The scorn of traditional values and the decline of family life are manifestations of these confusing times. As soon as practicable, I want to sell my company, gain financial security for my family, and pursue some worthwhile ambition: writing a book or two, playing tennis, traveling, and other things that will give meaning to my life.

President (40 to 49), construction company, Pennsylvania

The disparity between the social fiction and the social fact is so abundantly clear that you have underlined it with the use of the term "fiction." The primary cause for this disparity, in my opinion, is our refusal to adopt collective social programs in a specific and direct manner combined with legitimate demands for a higher degree of responsibility on the part of the administrators of these programs, the recipients, and the general public. Whether the program involves welfare, housing, education, the courts, the penal system, drugs, taxation, public service, the health of the economy, or any other activity area demanding collective effort, we preclude even reasonable success by approaching the problem politically or philosophically, partially or halfheartedly. Only through an overwhelming preoccupation with "pragmatism" grounded in truth (with due regard for individual aspirations) will we accomplish goals in areas requiring collective effort.

President (40 to 49), apparel holding company, New York

Yes, there is a growing disparity between the cultural mythology and the realities of life in America. Indications of this include increasing governmental intervention in the distribution of wealth (increasing social security collections, the coming national health insurance, federal poverty giveaway programs) and the expansion of a base of better-paid workers. I believe these activities—plus the rapidly escalating economy—put a stronger emphasis on the social fact. Moreover, today's young people are less interested in the so-called American Dream and are more oriented toward a life within the context and reality of the world as it exists today.

Executive (30 to 39), bank holding company, North Carolina

It is true that there are disparities between the mythology of the American Dream and how many people live their lives. Every once in a while, though, one meets an individual who is pursuing and achieving the American Dream: the businessman founding a company and bringing it to success; the professional person who achieves an honored position in his profession; the public official with an outstanding record of achievement. But there is still much that can be done in America: the development of more opportunities for young people, alleviation of extreme poverty, etc. One can walk the streets of any large city and see people who are merely existing, with no way to reach them except through rescue missions. These people exist outside the political and economic structure of our society.

Bookkeeper (50 to 59), manufacturing company, California

There may be a growing disparity, but at least there is a greater awareness of this disparity between the American Dream and the American reality. In wholesale lots, people are recognizing this disparity and feeling their own power to express themselves on the matter: the "Woodstock generation"; the Vietnam war protesters now saying, "I told you so"; the Nixon haters. It's not that these people are necessarily right in their beliefs, but they have learned how to speak up, to be heard, and to induce change. They see the present-day American condition without rose-colored glasses and are willing to speak up about what they see—warts and all. The warts have always been there (the "Negro" problem, for example), but out of concern and loving care, we are beginning to point them out and to talk about them.

Training manager (under 30), insurance company, Oregon

By paying a little attention to what people "say" and then noticing what they "do," one is bound to have some doubts about some of the "social fictions" in our society.

Internal auditor (50 to 59), state agency, New York

I support the view that there is a growing disparity between the social fiction and the social fact in American society today. The recently adopted social reform programs tend to put the burden on the hard-working, productive people in society in order to help the weak and, in many cases, the incompetent. Some of our welfare programs are, in my view, already overexpanded, inviting abuses and causing a dampening effect on people striving for reasonable rewards.

Engineer (40 to 49), multidivisional corporation, Massachusetts

I don't see a *growing* disparity, but then I feel that the gap has remained a wide one ever since the founding of our country. Racial prejudice is about as widespread and ingrained as ever in individuals in spite of the hollow lip service of recent EEO programs. Government in America does not respond to the individual citizen, but to large, monied pressure groups. The superwealthy in the United States continue to exert influence more in relation to their wealth than to their numbers. The wealthy seem to prosper in times of economic stress at the expense of others. Also, our leadership has not improved in honesty and morality over time.

Staff manager (40 to 49), industrial chemicals company, Ohio

There is and always has been a divergence between the social fiction and the social fact. Perhaps this should be stated in a different way: we have never fully achieved our aspirations. If we could do so, it would mean that our aspiration level was too low. We need goals—the "social fiction"—that we cannot reach. It is only in this way that we make slow progress toward improving the "social fact." The divergence is not a matter of hypocrisy as so many people claim. It is, instead, the spur to human improvement.

College professor (50 to 59), Pennsylvania

It is true that there is a widening gap between the American Dream and reality. It appears that the gap is widening because of the two basic groups of people in our society: the "older" generation that experienced the Depression and World War II and the

DELUSIONS

Our biggest delusion is that progress is free. Our forefathers sacrificed many things during the Industrial Revolution and through many wars. Their investment brought continual progress and a better way of life. Many people today believe that this place in the world is our "right" and that progress will continue without further investment. Our place in the world today really belongs to our fathers.

Data processing manager (under 30), building materials corporation, Washington

The biggest delusion in the United States and all the Western world is the Christian faith. Everywhere else, of course, we see that man has some form of religion. But man will be a truly modern being when he is able to throw off the emotional crutch of religion and face the complex problems of the world without the oversimplified, erroneous explanations and solutions offered by organized religion.

Marketing and sales director (30 to 39), pharmaceutical and chemical corporation, Pennsylvania

A single outstanding delusion—if not our biggest—is our tendency at present to fall into an imitative trap where obscenities have become the overriding veneer of our present-day culture. They claim to represent the facts of life by emphasizing the ugly, the sordid, and the unaesthetic aspects of our daily lives. This is not a true representation of humanity. It is another form of lying, another misuse of the tongue—although its advocates claim to be "telling it like it is." While obscenity tends to degrade him, man does not reach out for the true, the good, and the beautiful. Obscenity takes the experience of the moment and paints it as the whole. It ignores humanity's potentialities and lofty strivings. We all want to be uplifted. Let's avoid this trap, and if we have fallen into it, let's endeavor to get out.

Housewife (40 to 49), New York

The society in which we live tends to measure a person's success in terms of his or her economic advancement, power, and the prestige associated with a position. Some of this is important in a system that embraces a philosophy of growth, bigness, and improvement. I believe, however, that many people who achieve this kind of success fail to realize that real success may be a personal, inner satisfaction with respect to the "what," "how," and "why" of their efforts.

Administrator (30 to 39),
general hospital, Indiana

It is my opinion that our culture is deluded into believing that we live in a secular world and a secular society. Mr. Hal Lindsey, in his book The Late Great Planet Earth, *clears away some of the ideas that have deluded many.*

President (50 to 59), engineering
and design firm, North Carolina

We have deluded ourselves into polytheism as evidenced by the pedestals (salaries) we have allowed movie stars, top sports figures, and even politicians.

Personnel administrator (40 to 49),
manufacturing company, Idaho

The single biggest delusion in the United States today is the idea that inflation is not caused by wage increases in excess of productivity increases. Right now I feel that we need a law that wage increases cannot exceed the percent rise in the Consumer Price Index. This might help to allay inflation. Let's have no wage increases at all and let competition force prices down. This would help those on fixed incomes as well as the working population.

Vice president and group manager
(50 to 59), electronic equipment
manufacturing company, Kentucky

The biggest delusion with which we live today is the idea that we have a copyright on the best philosophy of life. The "missionary spirit"—that our way is the only way and that the savages must be saved—has been the basis for this philosophy.

Project leader (under 30), industrial
manufacturing company, Ohio

The biggest delusion to which Americans are subject is that fate, nature, or some omniscient force has decreed that we are a chosen people. This could be an innocent delusion if we did not insist on determining the form of government, degree of freedom, personal morality, and the economic system under which other people should live. Since World War II we have been attempting to buy friends and influence history through the largesse of our treasury. But there has been more enthusiasm and euphoria than reason and purpose in our giving.

President (50 to 59), food
brokerage company, Iowa

Americans today live under a delusion of freedom. The very foundation upon which our country is based is a delusion. Freedom simply does not exist unless we are free within ourselves. This means finding ourselves and knowing ourselves. This delusion of freedom exists because people know that such freedom does and should exist. But they do not realize that freedom must happen within themselves before it can be manifest externally in the world around them. We must be free within before we can be free without. How many of us are really free?

Respiratory therapist
(under 30), California

I believe that the single biggest delusion suffered by Americans is that ours is the best and only reasonable culture and form of government in the world. This leads us to believe that it is our obligation to export our way to the rest of the world, whether our way is suitable or not. The source of our delusion is in the chauvinistic treatment of our history in schools, patriotic and civic organizations, churches, and other social organizations. We propagan-

dize our children into believing that this is the best of all possible societies, with few, if any, faults, and that the rest of the world should aspire to be just like us. We point to our unparalleled prosperity as proof of this, operating on the premise that economic well-being is the be-all and end-all of human life.

Training and development director
(50 to 59), industrial
manufacturing company, Georgia

We have developed an overoptimism in this country about our ability to tackle and overcome any problems we might have to face. This delusion prevents us from seeing things in their proper perspective and from hearing (and believing) many of the social and economic warnings voiced by others.

Personnel director (30 to 39), steel
producing company, Pennsylvania

"younger" or "now" generation. The younger generation has little concept of the value of money and security. Young people are very mobile and feel free to "get up and go" as the mood strikes them—and with little regard for the future or concern for family and friends. The "older" generation is perhaps a little too conservative and values money in the bank and security too highly—thus the widening gap. Moral and social values follow a similar trend.

Technical services supervisor (50 to 59), industrial laboratory, California

When I was a high school senior, my family was the first in our community of about 2,500 people to be selected to house a foreign exchange student. We shared our home with a young West German girl my age but intellectually and educationally ahead of me. She was also very well versed in American education and teen-age life and believed in the idea that there was an American "well" that never dried up. As a newcomer to the United States, she was under the impression that things should just be given to her without her having to work for them.

My father was and still is an independent grocer. That year he had four children plus our mother to support. One just didn't get everything one wanted all the time around our house. It seems to me that the American condition has been misrepresented around the world. Through foreign eyes, the United States looks like a land of plenty, an easy grab. Maybe we are a land of relative plenty with great opportunities for the crowd. But things don't come easy or fast. That is the reality of the human experience in America today.

Personnel supervisor (under 30), financial management corporation, Maryland

I believe that there is a disparity between the social fiction and the social fact in this country, but I don't believe it's growing. There are many people working toward reducing this disparity—more people than ever—and with some success: Chavez, American Friends, and government programs such as EEO. It appears that a larger proportion of our younger people are structuring their lives around the American Dream—at least more seem

to be doing so than when I was their age. There is still much to be done in order to continue moving toward realization of the ideals expressed in the Bill of Rights. I hope that a majority of Americans will rededicate their lives during the bicentennial year toward achievement of the full meaning of our Declaration of Independence and the Bill of Rights.

Executive (50 to 59), pharmaceutical company, New Jersey

More and more we are becoming a "controlled" nation—controlled by an avalanche of laws, etc., in the social and professional sectors. "Bootstraps" are much harder to reach these days—EEO and OSHA, higher and higher taxes, and the cost of capital are examples. There are still opportunities for young dreamers in the service industries, but fewer and fewer in design and manufacturing. Goals are changing too. Why invest your cash and effort in a risky endeavor when you can do quite well by taking advantage of a series of government programs?

Staff manager (40 to 49), manufacturing company, North Carolina

I*s the American Dream a realization for the great majority of our people? Shouldn't we be grateful for the social progress we've already made? Were the "good old days" really all that good?*

I do not agree that there is a growing disparity between the social fiction and the social fact in American society today. We have in this country the highest standard of living in the world. We have mobility between various segments of our society. This is in contrast to other countries that have static societies in which one cannot move from one part of the country to another

without it being an unusual event. We have people living in this country making very high incomes and living on very high planes whose ancestors were savages 150 years ago. By "savages" I mean people living in jungle areas under a form of life that hadn't changed in thousands of years. We have people in the state of Iowa who came from homes with little educa-

tional background but who are today highly educated with a number of Ph.D.'s and M.D.'s in a single family. Going from a livery-stable helper to president of a university is the highest form of the American Dream. Of course, along the way you find people who are failures in one way or another—people who have cracked under the competition afforded by a

dynamic social and economic system. In Iowa we have a black man as bishop of the Methodist Church. Find me a Hindu religious hierarchy with a white man at the head. In this city, we have a black judge and—until she retired—a black representative in the state legislature. The population of my city is 7 percent black. There is a man up the street who is building a 36-story building which he will own when completed. He started out with one truck in 1934 and now has 4,000 of them plus this building and a bank. America is the greatest country in the world for material and cultural achievement.

President and treasurer (50 to 59), insurance company, Iowa

The American Dream has much meaning for most of our people. True, from time to time conditions change. We do experience periods of social upheaval and economic stress. By and large, however, the American Dream is a realization for the great majority of our people. No other society has brought to such a large percentage of its population the spiritual benefits of relative freedom and the material benefits of an unsurpassed standard of living. While critics can single out areas of less than satisfactory performance, on balance the dream continually comes true for most of our people. Who would really trade the "American Dream" for the "Russian Dream," or the "Swedish Dream," for that matter?

Vice president, corporate relations (50 to 59), appliance manufacturing company, Illinois

If you define the "American Dream" as "progress in developing each individual's control over his own life without creating chaos in society," then I believe the American condition is improving. On a comparative basis, either with the rest of the world or even with our own early history, we are making progress. Consider these inhibitors to human progress: Hunger—would anyone deny that the horror of this has been virtually eliminated in the United States? Health—are we not very close to providing broad availability of medical care to every economic level? Education—is this not readily available? According to statistics I have seen, a higher percentage of black Americans attend college than the percentage of all people attending college in France. We can do more, but isn't this progress? Economics—contrast the Depression and the panics of our early years with the recessions of today. Corruption—the press and Watergate, consumerism and business practices, ecological interests and the pollution of our environment. Everything is not "coming up roses." Love has not conquered all. But are we going backwards? Not where I live.

Vice president, operations (30 to 39), retail company, Ohio

I disagree that there is a growing disparity between the social fiction and the social fact. The "good old days" were hell. Today, I feel that the social fact is working toward the social fiction, if you wish to call it that. People, in general, have never had it so good and lack perspective with respect to what it was really like in the "good old days." However, their striving and bitching keeps the momentum rolling to close the gap even further. Just don't forget that the U.S.A. has the potential for anything. Most other countries, if not all, lack a social goal of working toward perfection.

Technical engineer (30 to 39), California

My *major delusion is acting optimistically in day-to-day affairs while little justification for this attitude exists. To me, it is dubious that men and women with sufficiently high ethical standards can be promoted to leadership positions in this society in time to forestall societal collapse. Greed, waste, and population growth are accelerating the decline of America.*

Technical manager (under 30), industrial corporation, New York

The single biggest delusion with which we Americans live today is the notion of individual independence. In my opinion, there is entirely too much teaching about what the individual can do "if he sets his mind to it." I believed that notion when I first heard it, and tried it, but my life did not provide any personal satisfaction until I gave up my "independence" and began to work in conjunction with the power of the Holy Spirit. I believe that all greatness is rooted in God. When we as individuals or as a nation attribute greatness in our lives to ourselves rather than to God, we are beginning to construct our own coffins.

Executive vice president (30 to 39), commercial bank, Virginia

We Americans like to imagine that because of our generally high standard of living, military might, and global influence, we are invincible. History shows that all great cultures, nations, and civilizations eventually tumble. We must grasp and accept this reality and learn from history. A great and mighty nation such as ours does not easily accept the idea of a fall. But we are deluding ourselves until we do accept this fact and use it to our advantage for as long as we can.

Assistant vice president, government relations (40 to 49), insurance company, Michigan

Today's Americans are deluded by the American Dream. If realized, the American Dream may mean material

What about our personal dreams and disappointments? A few of us responded to a question that asked us to assess the extent to which our own lives and aspirations have worked out as planned. Frankly, we believe our track record is pretty good, on balance.

My own life has worked out as I have planned it—in the range of 40 to 60 percent. There wasn't much planning in terms of a written program, so to speak, but I have relied on thought and an intuitive planning approach. In general, my life has worked out more on the happy side (rather than the gloomy side) in that I have felt fulfilled by some of my accomplishments and the wonderful associations I have had with other people. These have been my good fortune. An example of life defeating a personal aspiration involves the failure of my own general contracting business after eight years of great effort and financial difficulty. But in all honesty, one can only lay the responsibility to one's own handling of various situations. The responsibility for the company's failure was my own.

Physical plant director
(50 to 59), Maryland university

I don't believe that my generation did much planning for our lives. We knew that we had to have a job and believed that if we worked, the rewards would come to us and would offset any temporary setbacks or disappointments we might experience. Without planning, I would say that I have attained a level that is higher than I probably would have settled for when I graduated college in 1935. At 62 years of age, I am really quite happy with the results achieved for the steady, long pull that I have had to make in the so-called rat race.

Vice president and general
manager (60 or over),
finance company, Pennsylvania

In general, my life has worked out pretty much as I planned it. I was coming of age in the Great Depression years and it taught me a couple of things: first, that very little in this life is really free, and, second, that whatever I accomplished in life was going to be done by hard work and not by a great deal of talent. I suppose that my greatest disappointment was being refused an officer's commission in World War II because of a minor physical ailment.

Vice president and chief engineer
(60 or over), Illinois company

There was very little planning in my life except to become professionally qualified to work in my field. A large part of what has happened to me has come about by taking advantage of an unusual opportunity that came my way. My dream in my mid-twenties was to become a millionaire. When I realized the sacrifice involved, I decided it wasn't worth it. As time goes on, money becomes less and less important to me.

Management consultant
(30 to 39), California

My life is very different from the way I might have planned it. I actually did very little concrete thinking about my future. I went to college because I was intelligent but couldn't "do" anything. I got married because I was in love. I expected that my life would be very much like my mother's—I would keep house and raise a family. Instead I am a career woman today. I am divorced and my life style is very different from that of my parents. I believe *security, but left hanging out there is moral and spiritual embellishment. Americans live from one day to the next, grasping for the ring, never fully realizing that the "Dream" is mostly a sham—at best, a bait.*

Personnel director (30 to 39), chemical corporation, Ohio

Our biggest national delusion, in my opinion, is that we can have the most affluent society the world has ever known, without working for it. Exactly how this has come about is difficult to phrase. It is a combination of many things: permissiveness, technological development, population mobility, union power, more creature comforts, and a love of ease and luxury that has led to laziness. Regrettably, it may take a major depression to bring people to their senses.

Vice president, government affairs (50 to 59), multinational food manufacturing company, Connecticut

We are deluded by the notion that affluence is automatic and that because it is automatic it is not necessary to make a contribution to our government or to society to assure that the American way of free enterprise continues to function.

Executive vice president (30 to 39), electronic services company, Texas

Many, too many, people believe that we can continue to enjoy the "good life" without paying the price. This was my personal belief in earlier years. But we as a nation and part of a new world society must understand this simple fact: recent economic experience shouts out that we cannot continue in our past ways. We just have to face the real world, set new priorities, and understand that we cannot purchase all that we want or think we need.

Senior vice president (40 to 49), insurance company, Massachusetts

We are deluded with the notion that we can get something for nothing.

Quality control manager (60 or over), automotive industry, Illinois

Our biggest delusion is the notion that there is a well that has no bottom.

Personnel director (50 to 59), food products manufacturing company, Michigan

Our biggest delusion is the idea that the world owes us a living.

Training manager (age not indicated), chemical distribution company, California

Our biggest delusion is that "right" will win eventually and that people who work hard and are honest will get their just reward. In the United States it is the dishonest and the crooked who get rewarded. Our society is wicked and seems to be getting worse. Business is probably the source of this delusion, along with our love of wealth and material things, regardless of the cost. We work on people's greed. Our only salvation is through Jesus Christ and our love of our fellow men. Without this love, we will destroy ourselves. Until this nation realizes where it has gone wrong, we will continue to decay until destroyed.

Plant engineer (40 to 49), automobile manufacturing company, Michigan

The biggest mass delusion in American society today is the idea of a "free lunch." That is, our expectations in many areas of our national life exceed our ability to produce. This mass delusion is caused in part by the nature of democracy, wherein it is good politics to exploit this delusion. It then feeds on itself. It is also caused by the achievements we have experienced to date. It would take a national emergency of catastrophic proportions (real or imagined) to shatter this delusion.

President (40 to 49), food services corporation, Georgia

my life and life style are different from what I planned in the 1950s because the world is a different place to live in now. There is much more emphasis on individual achievement and personal satisfaction—at least I emphasize these in my own personal life.

Business librarian (30 to 39),
public library, California

Everything has worked out exactly as I wanted to imagine years ago—perhaps more so. However, my lack of formal or professional education has hindered my progress. In addition to the responsibility for putting three children through college—and a fourth will start college next year—I have had to take care of my husband, who is unable to work. All of this has increased the pressure on me to perform. But this is where it's at, and I would do it all again. And where but here in America would I have the opportunity?

Assistant business manager
(40 to 49), school
district, Illinois

My life has generally been highly satisfactory, interesting, and challenging. All of my major goals have been met, with one very important exception. The sale and merger of my company has proven to be very unsatisfying. In the several years since the merger, I have learned that the company I merged with has an entirely different set of ethics from my own. The parent firm is intensely arrogant, self-centered, and not at all people-oriented. Furthermore, the parent company operates on the basis that a contract is a license to steal, and let the buyer beware. As a result of this association, my own image in my industry has been tarnished, and mine is an industry in which I was a pioneer. Responsibility for this defeat rests entirely on my shoulders, as I should have investigated the suitor company more thoroughly. In retrospect, while I would never again consider an association with this firm, I have learned a great deal about how to investigate a

company so as not to fall into a similar trap again. I have also been made aware of the true strength of my own preferred position in any situation of stress. Hence, I have to view the overall situation as a learning experience.

Division president (40 to 49),
West Coast company

I have been very fortunate and my life has worked out pretty much as planned and hoped for. Being drafted after school and after marriage was [somewhat] bad, but not all bad. I do not begrudge the time spent serving my country.

Director of operations
(30 to 39), frozen
food manufacturing
company, North Dakota

I had two goals in life: one, to manage or direct a factory, and, two, to command a battalion in the National Guard. In October 1968, I was appointed general manager of the firm I have worked for since 1964. In

January 1974 I was designated battalion commander for the area National Guard organization. Life has never defeated me. I have only myself to blame for those occasions when I did suffer defeat. I didn't work hard enough.

Manager (40 to 49),
cigar manufacturing
company, Puerto Rico

As far as my life is concerned, since I put myself through night law school, things have worked out pretty well. That is, until the last 30 days or so. Due to a change in company presidents—which was forced by a change in the principal ownership of the company—I and the company I have worked so hard to make successful these past five years are going to part in a few months. The net result to me may be positive, but for now it is extremely disappointing.

General counsel (40 to 49),
computer manufacturing
company, California

The technological advances of the past 75 years combined with the exploitation of the vast resources of our land has led to our people believing—particularly those under 45 years of age—that the good things of a material nature are going to be theirs forever with a minimum of work and effort on their part.

President and board
chairperson (60 or over),
public utility, Nevada

Too many Americans seem to feel that others are responsible for them, that the government owes life support to everyone, and that there will always be someone else to do the job and pay the bills. Educational programs must be developed—and some support programs must be curtailed—for the purpose of teaching people once again the true meaning of democracy, of free enterprise, and of the need for individual participation in work and play to accomplish the goals people have set for themselves. Not everyone will have everything, but those who make personal efforts can achieve a great many of their goals.

Vice president, administration
(40 to 49), financial
services company, Wisconsin

We delude ourselves by thinking that our resources are unlimited. We have preached this gospel around the globe through such things as the Peace Corps. Now we find it isn't true, and we are having a hard time realizing that there are limits. The big question is: Can we discipline and contain our use of resources?

Chief executive officer
(50 to 59), manufacturing
company, Minnesota

We think, mistakenly, that natural resources are inexhaustible and that there is a technological solution to every environmental problem, no matter how severe. The source of these delusions is related to the expansionist philosophy carried over from the last century and beginning of this one. The

solution is for every American (and for all people everywhere, for that matter) to adopt the philosophy of stewardship toward the planet and all its resources. The survival of the human species will require taking a long-term view. Unfortunately, I see little evidence that the typical American (especially businessmen) can see beyond next year's profits or the five-year market plan.

Research group manager
(30 to 39), Illinois company

In my opinion, the most prominent of the delusions we Americans live with today is that shortages of raw materials which we are experiencing will go away—that the shortages have been artificially created. The basis for this delusion is in the belief that there are always new frontiers and that modern technology is able to perform miracles. The only way to dispel this delusion for many people rests in the hard, cold fact of continued shortages. Continued efforts to educate people about the need to conserve would be preferable and will reach the thinking public over a period of time.

Director of nursing services
(50 to 59), private
hospital, Colorado

Americans delude themselves and create their own frustrations and disappointments by continually confusing words—declarations of intent, slogans, and emotional posturing—with effective, goal-oriented action. By simply declaring, for example, a "War on Poverty," many of us are led to believe that all perceived personal economic problems will evaporate.

Assistant group controller
(30 to 39), food
manufacturing company, Ohio

America's biggest delusion is that complex problems can be solved in a short time and be put behind us. Initial waves of concern (new laws, demonstrations, and even wars) focus attention on problems, but in a few years

Life is change, and few things, if any, remain constant. How has our experience changed our lives, our self-concept and self-awareness? Do we ever deceive ourselves with respect to "who" or "what" we are? These are not easy questions to answer.

Ten years ago, I determined my life according to what society dictated. By "society," I mean those people from whom I could get immediate feedback. They would mold my behavior. They smoked; I smoked. They drank; I drank. They bought new cars; so did I (even if I couldn't really afford to). In plain English, I had no self. Now I do what I please, within legal limits. I like to be admired by others; therefore, I try to remain cheerful and positive and to display as much tact as possible. I do this knowingly and I love it. Do I deceive myself? Absolutely! Usually I deceive myself about my age. Maybe I deceive myself less and less with each new gray hair and wrinkle, but I continue to go on pretending because it feels good to feel young.

Placement director (30 to 39), Texas business college

My self-awareness and self-concept have changed significantly during the past ten years. I used to believe that I was put here on this earth to contribute in some small way to the unfolding of a much larger scheme. Money and material things were only important to me as a means of acquiring the essentials of life. There was a deep concern for others less fortunate. How have I changed? The more money I make, the greater the financial support I am giving to the government for redistribution to people who aren't self-supporting. My concept has changed in the sense that I now put more effort into defending my right to be paid more money and less effort into the quality of the work I must do to pro-

duce a quality product. I no longer feel that I am part of a team or that I work in a "professional" capacity. The most logical reason I can give for feeling this way now is related to the fact that "work" has become a dirty word. We can no longer express our true feelings to the people we work with. We are overprotected by regulations—both externally and internally imposed.

Manager, technical services field (40 to 49), state government, Michigan

Ten years ago I felt I was receiving no breaks in life and that the ends pretty well justified the means. I have now pretty well reversed this trend and attempt to treat all people as decently as possible and to give everyone the benefit of the doubt in my dealings with them. Saying "thank you" and "please" at all times is more and more essential in business every day. The building of trust in day-to-day relationships with people is basically more important to me today than anything else.

Purchasing agent (30 to 39), farm machinery company, North Dakota

I delude myself with respect to "who" and "what" I am because it is what is expected of a person in my role. My superiors hold me in high regard—higher than most—yet I continually sense the nonrealization of my potential or even real-world accomplishments. Until four years ago, I knew myself as the person playing the role. About that time I realized that I was "acting out my play." About one year ago I further realized the futility of our moral codes—although until then I was most inflexible in my moral code. Still, my role-playing keeps me from walking barefoot in the sand all day.

Project officer (40 to 49),
U.S. Navy, Virginia

I do feel there has been a change in my self-awareness in recent years. Frankly, I feel better about myself now than I did as a youth. I now realize that I was too much achievement-oriented and extremely threatened by the fear of failure. One big delusion was to draw my self-esteem from my accomplishments—honor student, responsible job with a large New York City corporation, etc. The immensity of that corporation and of the city has made me see how small and unimportant I am. This was disappointing at first, but now I somehow feel stronger and more self-aware. I now know that my pride must be pride in my personhood and that my importance is based on what I can understand of the human condition and the friendships I might make.

Executive secretary (under 30),
social welfare
organization, New York

the attention shifts to another problem without our having attained a reasonable solution to the other ones. The net result is often poorly developed and short-range solutions, with many problems remaining troublesome.

Personnel executive (50 to 59), consumer products company, Ohio

We continue to believe in the existence of a free-market economy. What's wrong is that our industries are much too large. They've grown beyond the bounds of competitive forces, primarily because the Justice Department has not vigorously enforced antitrust laws. Any company whose individual fortunes (good or bad) can affect the entire economy is too big and should be broken up.

Management consultant (30 to 39), California

The biggest American delusion is the concept of a free enterprise system. Oil cartels, automotive cartels, food cartels, etc., are ripping off the American consumer, while the small businessman—the symbol of free enterprise—is being disenfranchised. The breakup of big business may hurt economically in the short run, but will be better for America in the long run—economically, politically, and socially.

Executive (40 to 49), communications industry, District of Columbia

Many Americans think that we are surrounded by limitations—limitations which prevent the practical realization of success, happiness, prosperity, peace, etc. In many cases we impose

the limitations on ourselves by restricting reasoning. Where do we draw the line and say that limitations are in some cases real and in other cases just a delusion or a lack of perception of opportunity? To what extent are limitations real? Are limitations ever real?

Data processing analyst
(30 to 39), state
government, California

Our biggest delusion is that America is a land of plenty, when, in fact, we neither have nor control sources of raw materials for energy and for essential industrial needs basic to our economy. The delusion is a carryover from an earlier time in our history when the idea that we had an abundance of raw materials was essentially true.

Assistant vice president,
operations (50 to 59),
retail chain, Pennsylvania

Today we believe that we can continue to expand our luxury base with an ever-decreasing emphasis on securing the basic necessities of life—food, shelter, and clothing. Our value system has become our greatest delusion. We need to reexamine it. This is not a limitless-supply world, but we seem to be willing to view it as such.

Vice president and general
manager (50 to 59),
farm equipment company, Ohio

A big delusion that we face is that America can continue to support its current standard of living while ignoring pressures from the rest of the world. Our growing dependency on other nations—especially with respect to raw materials—will require a greater sense of partnership than was previously needed. It will also require that that partnership be on terms not necessarily to our liking. We will be [forced] to accept a less dominant role in many world affairs. At the same time we may be asked to go on supporting most of the world's needs. In our new world position, we will be effective, but in ways different from those of the past.

Plant manager (40 to 49),
chemical company, New York

Our biggest delusion is that government can cure all social and economic ills in our society. The previous generation felt that sweatshops, migrant labor, massive unemployment, depression, lack of medical care, etc., were facts of life—something we all had to live with. While it has been shown that man, working together, can solve these problems, the delusion now is that we as citizens no longer have to contribute, that somehow the government will do it. The idea that government is us and not our protector will require some hard rethinking. While I am optimistic, patterns of thinking die hard. Witness the centuries: long beliefs in dogma and ritual which comforted so many generations of our forefathers through constant hell, pestilence, famine, petty wars, etc. In a way, government today has replaced old-time religion as a panacea.

Civilian analyst (40 to 49),
Department of the Army, Virginia

Our biggest delusion is the idea that the government will take care of us—come what may. The cure for this delusion is obvious. We need to reassert the Christian ethic.

Manager of labor relations
and personnel (50 to 59),
manufacturing plant, Missouri

It is my feeling that the greatest delusion in existence today is that the federal government is the source of all knowledge, wisdom, power, and money. We all seem to think that there is some magic on the banks of the Potomac that can solve all problems, both for us as individuals and for our society and the entire world. We are deluding ourselves when we think these things. Any time we face a problem, we don't look within ourselves for answers but to Washington. Self-reliance in this country and throughout the world is a lost art.

Vice president, personnel
(50 to 59), transportation
company, North Carolina

Our biggest delusion is that our country is falling to pieces and that nothing here is any good. Even with Watergate and economic, social, and moral conditions as they are, there's no place in the world like the good old U.S.A. as a place to live.

Executive and procurement
director (50 to 59),
engineering firm, New Jersey

We think we have the obligation and the resources to take care of the rest of the world. Stupidity is responsible for this delusion.

Accountant (40 to 49),
manufacturing company, Georgia

Many people today claim that our country is in the grip of widespread moral, ethical, and spiritual decay. Most of us agree with this assessment of our national condition and want to talk here about some of the reasons for the deterioration we perceive and what we believe can be done to reverse this destructive course. Some of us foresee a change for the better in the moral and spiritual climate in America, noting *other* forces in our national life that we believe are working to restore wholesome human values and right human behavior.

Concurrence with the foregoing, as might be expected, is not universal, and a few of us are just as certain that moral, ethical, and spiritual conditions in America today are not nearly as bad as they seem. Also, while many of our ideas about moral and spiritual conduct may be changing, some of us believe that these changes need not always imply the loss of something good. In fact, many of the changes that we see all around us may be for the better—though the opposite may seem true at first glance.

What, then, are some of the factors in our national life that we believe contribute to a degeneration in the moral and spiritual fiber of our times? Can it be, to begin with, that we Americans—or many of us, at least—are too materialistic, too affluent, too attached to the ''almighty dollar'' for our own moral, ethical, and spiritual good? Some of us clearly think so.

ETHICS, MORALITY, AND SPIRITUAL VALUES

I believe we *are* in the grip of an ethical, moral, and spiritual decline in American society. This is evidenced by the importance that has been placed on the almighty dollar and how it can be earned with the least amount of effort. The moral decline that hurts business the most is the attitude among workers that unions will protect their jobs. A commonly accepted philosophy among workers today is, ''Why should I work eight hours for eight hours of pay?'' This attitude has led to a slowdown in output both by individuals and by work groups. This slowdown has become accepted practice in American industry. Management needs to again concentrate on increasing worker productivity for the high salaries employees now receive. Management must also establish in the public mind the right and the need to make a profit.

Consulting engineer (40 to 49),
construction industry, Illinois

Our moral decline has resulted from an overemphasis on financial security and materialism and from a breakdown of the family unit as a force in the early establishment of sound value systems for children. I hear some expression of concern among our leaders but do not see enough concern being expressed by people generally to bring about a significant change. I believe that the situation will have to deteriorate to the point where there will be wide recognition of the need to reassess our value systems.

Chief executive (60 or over),
agricultural bank, Kansas

The United States is in a moral, ethical, and spiritual decline brought about by an abundant way of life and a welfare system that destroys personal ambition and dignity. The attitude that the world owes one a living does not foster reliance on one's own abilities and the need for Divine assistance. An abundant way of life leads to excesses of every manner, and these excesses weaken the moral and ethical fiber of

the people. In addition, abundance and excessive indulgence reduce an individual's awareness of spiritual needs. Morality suffers as a result of our exposure to the mass media distribution of, at best, marginal entertainment, especially when the individual hasn't had any moral and spiritual upbringing to begin with. I foresee a steady erosion of all the values that made this country great.

Executive (30 to 39),
manufacturing company, Illinois

I believe that our tremendous desire for material wealth and pleasures spurred by television, advertising, and personal expectations resulting from better education is the main factor responsible for the moral and spiritual decline we are in. This insatiable desire for pleasure and possession seems to be increasing, and I don't foresee any turnaround. Nothing short of national adversity or widespread dramatic personal change will bring us back to a higher level of morality and spiritual practice. I must admit to being a part of the general decline—and I don't feel capable of fighting the tide. Perhaps I had better make the effort, however. Somebody must try. Perhaps if enough individuals try hard enough, we can make some progress.

Manpower planning manager
(40 to 49), steel producing
company, Ohio

I agree that we are in a moral decline. Our schools and the media seem to glorify the success of lumpish louts who can kick or throw a ball and to equate mental ability with failure. The contributions to society made by professional athletes and entertainers are out of all proportion in relation to the huge monetary rewards they receive. Obviously, this is only a symptom, but one that is typical of the extremely warped sense of values in our country today. Our greed for material things may well be our downfall.

General manager (40 to 49),
lumber products
company, Arkansas

I do believe that we are in the grip of an ethical, moral, and spiritual decline due mainly to a long period of prosperity during which most Americans were able to acquire everything they wanted with no fear whatsoever of going deeply into debt. Our prosperity has led us to emphasize social life and to deemphasize the church and Deity. Unemployment, hardship, and difficulty will cause Americans to return to true worship. We could become a Christian nation again.

Group vice president (40 to 49),
food products company, Arizona

I think that the greatest force that is contributing to our decline is our materialistic concept of life. Our materialistic philosophy has led us to believe that we are masters of everyone and everything we come in contact with. We believe that there is no higher creature or creator than ourselves. This notion is fostered by technology and by our ability to control the use of things and people in this world. We do not recognize that there is a higher power, God. If we did recognize this, we would also realize that all people have the same basic rights and responsibilities. A few philosophers are saying that for this to occur, there must be a reconciliation of all created things with their creator. This means that all created things, including human beings, need to recognize God as their creator and as the ultimate being. In recognizing that there is a God who is our creator, we would recognize principles of morality; we would recognize that we have a certain length and depth of life and a meaningful existence on this earth. Belief in God as creator would bring us back to some of the realities of the principles of the brotherhood of man—the principles that we must uphold if we are to retain the brotherhood of man.

Hospital administrator
(40 to 49), Ohio

The wealth that has come our way by the exploitation of resources—particularly energy—has weakened our moral fiber generally and the moral character of our leadership. As our resources diminish and as environmental problems become inescapable, natural law will dictate the rebuilding of a stronger, more honest and moral soci-

ety. Our survival will require it. It is difficult to see this happening without widespread turmoil. Hopefully the situation will not be cataclysmic.

Corporate planner (40 to 49),
nondurable goods
company, Michigan

Materialism has contributed to our moral decline. People have forgotten God. They try to find happiness in sin. Also, the trend toward socialism or "governmentism" takes the sense of initiative away from members of the lower classes. They reason, "Why should I work hard to succeed? Let the government help me." Unless our country returns to the fundamentals on which it was based ("In God we trust") the United States will become another lost empire for the history books—like Rome and Greece, and so many others.

Division controller (40 to 49),
electronic components manufacturing
company, South Carolina

*S*ome of us believe that our leaders are failing to provide sound moral leadership and that lack of ethics in high places is widespread. Some fault an inadequate judicial system and a number of recent judicial decisions that affect the lives of us all. Others suspect that the "largeness" or "unresponsiveness" of many of our institutions contributes substantially to moral deterioration. Finally, a few feel that we have lost respect for one another and even for life itself.

The moral decline in our society stems, for the most part, from our political and social leaders having yielded to the pressures of special interest groups. Once we were a society with strong and stable ethical, moral, and spiritual standards—a society that rewarded the producer, that cared for those not capable of producing, that trained those who wanted to produce but lacked the necessary

skills, and that respected people with different opinions or spiritual convictions. Now we seem to have no stable standards. We overtax the producer, reward the nonproducer, and deny the right of competition on the rationale of equalization. I do not foresee a change for the better in the near future. The forces that could prompt such a change would have to be so severe as to jolt our scholars, business leaders, politi-

"Our moral decline has resulted from an overemphasis on financial security and materialism and from a breakdown of the family unit as a force in the early establishment of sound value systems for children."

Dishonesty and lack of ethics at high levels of government have led to a decline in the moral and spiritual fiber of our country. A president, a vice president, cabinet officers, and others have practiced deceit and have misused public trust. This is more prevalent in this period of history than in the past, and citizens are frustrated, suspicious, frightened, and depressed because of this misuse of trust. Perhaps in the long run the events of the past few years will provide the incentive to improve our moral and spiritual behavior. We have experienced the agony that corruption can cause. But I am optimistic. Our country will survive and grow stronger.

Executive (50 to 59), agricultural supply cooperative, Ohio

I believe we are in the grip of an ethical, moral, and spiritual decline in American society. Some of the factors responsible for this include inadequate leadership at all levels and in all sectors of society, public indifference, laziness, and personal greed. People today seem to care only about themselves and their own possessions and immediate personal welfare. I do not foresee a change for the better. Much higher-quality leadership at all levels is needed, and perhaps a real, all-encompassing national emergency requiring sacrifice and causing a drastic change in people's lives will be the only way positive change will come.

Supervisor (30 to 39), U.S. law enforcement agency, Virginia

I agree that American society is experiencing an ethical, moral, and spiritual decline. The forces that have contributed most to this decline include the leadership of our educational institutions, churches, labor unions, corporations, and the government. Also there has been an excessive degree of liberalism in the life styles of our college youth during the past ten years—influenced by a lack of discipline in our schools, a relaxing of

church dogma (in an attempt to retain members), and an obsession with the pursuit of pleasure and "hand-outs," without responsible efforts on the part of the individual. While I feel that a change for the better is in progress, the process will be a slow one unless something happens soon (like a depression to jolt our sense of values) to restore respect for work and individual accomplishment.

Vice president (50 to 59), public warehouse company, Massachusetts

I believe we are in the grip of a moral decline caused primarily by the unforeseen results of the Supreme Court decisions of the 1950s and 1960s with respect to the rights of individuals and minority groups. Concern for the individual has taken precedence over concern for the good of society. The Supreme Court's decisions have unexpectedly given rise to what amounts to anarchy on the part of individuals and minorities. Law and order has broken down, with law enforcement officers being almost as inhibited by the laws as are criminals. Government officials are censured or forced to resign because of off-the-cuff remarks considered offensive to minority groups. Unions have become all-powerful and contribute to inflation by rarely equating wage demands with increased

cians, and the news media back to reality. We need to join in a united effort to promote good old Americanism: accepting the responsibility that accompanies every right and privilege; being willing to sacrifice in the face of need; being concerned for others; and respecting other people's views and convictions.

Personnel manager (40 to 49), industrial equipment company, Indiana

The biggest cause of moral and ethical decline in this country has been the out-and-out defiance of the law on the part of our elected officials (income tax evasion, etc.). The motion picture and television industries have also contributed to the problem—with TV having more of an impact because it comes right into the home. Our spiritual decline is the result of an age of permissiveness—many of the old values of the past are now looked upon as phony. I do not foresee a change for the better, but change must come, or our society is in real trouble. I believe that we must be more selective in who we elect to political office. If our politicians betray our trust, we must get them out. We need a real leader—one who is an honest, "grass roots" American.

Distribution manager (50 to 59), food products company, Minnesota productivity. Corporate greed worships at the shrine of profits and at the expense of the consumer and society. The new anarchy of the individual and the minorities will probably run its course during the next 50 years, and will leave as its legacy a new society, the form of which defies speculation at this time. We can only hope that our sons and daughters—as they suffer through the transition—will sow the seeds of a new and more relevant society for future generations.

Vice president, development
(50 to 59), pharmaceutical
company, Connecticut

I support the notion that we are experiencing a moral, ethical, and spiritual decline. I believe that the Supreme Court decision against prayer in schools has had a great deal to do with it. At the present time, I see no portent for change for the better in the moral, ethical, or spiritual climate of our times.

Vice president, sales
(50 to 59), petroleum products
company, New York

I believe we are in a moral decline. We have an inadequate judicial system. We have done away with capital punishment. Hardened criminals are turned loose to commit more crimes. Our democracy is great, but it demands leadership, which is at its lowest ebb in all my 52 years. Morally and spiritually our great country is bleeding to death—Mr. Mills versus Fanne Foxe, Mr. President versus Watergate. Pornographic materials can be found everywhere by our children—on radio, TV, and in print. Leadership, integrity, and loyalty must be demonstrated by our elected officials. We must all get away from being Democrats or Republicans and vote for the individual. The clergy needs a good shake-up too. The clergy is the culprit in many instances of moral decline and poor leadership.

Personnel manager (50 to 59),
lumber products
manufacturing company, Florida

We are in a moral and ethical decline. The primary reason, as I see it, is the largeness of American institutions. Bigness breeds lack of control. People receive security from big organizations and begin to think that anything is OK as long as they don't get caught.

Services coordinator (30 to 39),
religious youth group, Colorado

Faceless, impersonal, and unresponsive institutions in our society have forced our present culture to retreat to the suicidal practice of self-centered hedonism in order to retain a measure of individual identity and pride. The average individual feels frustrated and helpless in his inability to exert influence over the many institutions that govern his daily life. As a result, people are now rejecting those institutions that have rejected them and are turning within themselves for fulfillment of such basic human needs as love, attention, and recognition. The pursuit of self-love, self-indulgence, and self-interest have attained paramount importance, as these objectives are entirely egocentric and do not require the cooperation of society and its institutions. This distrust of our institutions has also led to a rejection of authority and leadership at all levels. "Do your own thing" has become more important than "Do unto others as you would have them do unto you." It is fashionable to be "liberated" from morals, tradition, and responsibility to anyone but oneself. This egocentric, hedonistic philosophy may eventually lead us to a chaotic state of anarchy. To prevent this, we must breathe new life into all our institutions. We must decentralize and humanize them. We must make them listen and respond to the needs, desires, and opinions of our people. We must ask the people within these institutions to reassert such basic human characteristics as concern, appreciation, kindness, morality, responsibility, and commitment. If we are to function as complete human beings, we cannot allow our identities to be submerged in mindless, lifeless corporate or governmental structures. Decision-making responsibilities and authority must be delegated to the lowest possible levels in the organization. As individuals, we must get out of ourselves, respond to the needs of others, and again see what it is like to make someone else happy.

Business manager (30 to 39),
medical care group, Texas

Yes, morals are declining. We have lost the meaning of the word respect—respect for parents, elders, courts, the church, law and order, and honesty. To improve the situation, our politicians, educators, and the news media must set better examples for others to follow.

President (60 or over),
insurance agency, Connecticut

So many factors have contributed to the moral, ethical, and spiritual decline in America that it is difficult to pinpoint the one factor most responsible. The great emphasis in recent years on allowing a person the right to do his own thing has been corrupted into a philosophy that allows a person to do anything. There seem to be few restraints on what people can say and do. I believe that the use of foul language and the so-called four-letter words (and other vivid descriptions of the sexual act) together with the promiscuity that prevails among people of all ages today has been a large contributing factor to moral decline. Modern novels are an abhorrence because they seem to focus on the idea that everyone—regardless of his or her status in society—participates in free love either with a neighbor, a neighbor's wife, or anyone who might be handy. We are bombarded today with every indication that sex is the paramount thing. We see this in advertising on TV and in all the short stories and modern novels that lead readers into thinking that this is the "norm" in a good society.

I believe this is wrong and should be stopped. People should exercise some restraint when preparing this kind of material for publication. Of course, the world is aware of all the lying, cheating, and stealing that go on, and it is very difficult to teach young people that this behavior is wrong when they see it happening every day. All of this lying, stealing, and cheating

has led to more violence in the streets to support a drug or alcohol habit—or just to have enough money to keep up with peers. It is time that we show some restraint and get back to what has been described as "graceful living," where we respect our neighbor and his rights and do not exercise our rights to the detriment of those with whom we have to live.

Corporate accountant (50 to 59),
mining company, Georgia

Any society that sanctions abortion and that is more concerned for the criminal than for the victims of crime is declining morally and spiritually. Life is held in low regard today, when it is permissible to kill unborn babies up to 26 weeks old, but not permissible to execute criminals who murder people or groups of people. We live in a permissive society with no overall standards of right and wrong. If abortion is permissible, then why not "euthanasia" for those over age 65 or

for the handicapped? These people, too, like some unborn children, are not "convenient" for us to have around.

Personnel director (40 to 49),
consumer goods company,
New Jersey

I feel that an important underlying factor in our moral and ethical decline is a governmental system that has become too unwieldy and inertia-bound to meet the needs of society. I feel the decline parallels a breakdown in our judicial system, which has fostered a decline in the ethics and morals of people in government, in groups and associations, and in individuals. I do not foresee a change for the better. A change for the better will occur only as a result of success in the strict application of the rules of society and when swift, consistent punishment is administered to all offenders.

Manager of research and
engineering (40 to 49),
capital equipment
manufacturing company, Kansas

T*he factors contributing to a weakening in the moral and spiritual fiber of our times are many and varied, in the view of a large number of us.*

We are experiencing a moral and ethical decline because our courts have failed to punish wrongdoers, because government officials and the general public have catered too much to well-organized pressure groups, because of the growth of idealism, which ignores the need to compromise ideals at times in order to provide the greatest good for the greatest number of people, and finally because we have tried to correct social wrongs through revolutionary rather than evolutionary means.

Mergers and acquisitions manager
(50 to 59), Ohio company

Any individual or civilization that worships false gods ends in disaster. When we ignore true and proven

standards, sooner or later we receive the penalty. America deserves what has occurred these past few years. We have lost control in our country. We tend to rationalize our situation as being beyond the individual's control. We have adopted irresponsible attitudes. Individual greed, government ineffectiveness, corporate corruption, and other signs of disintegration are everywhere. Americans are beginning to show signs of middle age at only 25 or 26 years of age. Obesity today demands that stadium seats be 3 inches wider than before World War II. Thirty-one percent of all American women admit to being overweight while people starve to death in Asia. We have broken fundamental Judeo-

Christian laws. We have been living beyond our means, spending more than we earn, engaging in immoral practices, and now we will have to pay the penalty. By reducing our expenditures and our standard of living, by voluntarily aiding the needy, by investing more time and effort in our youth, and by returning to the time-proven principles of our heritage, the situation will improve. If we don't do these things, we will destroy ourselves. It's as simple as that. We have overcome other difficulties in the past, and we will conquer this one. The road back will require a lot of individual effort. Let's not try to minimize the difficulty. America will never be the same again—and after what we've experienced these past few years, maybe that's a blessing.

Recruiting and training director (40 to 49), information systems industry, Oklahoma

The events of the past few years—politics (Watergate), the courts (abortion on demand), business (payoffs and political contributions in excess of the law, spurious financial reports, etc.)—lead me to believe that we are becoming lax and complacent with respect to the moral, ethical, and spiritual aspects of life. We need to demand a higher standard of performance in these areas. Life has become too easy, and I am sorry to say that maybe we need a recession (possibly a depression) to bring us back to what we know is right.

Management consultant (40 to 49), health institutions, Nebraska

Mankind, in my opinion, has been, is, and always will be basically selfish. But in America today there exists an atmosphere in which the restraining forces on selfishness are being weakened while those that foster selfish behavior are being enhanced. Population growth is another problem. It has produced cities in which impersonal relationships between people are the ''norm,'' in which friction is commonplace, resulting in bad man-

ners at best and violence at worst. Scientific advances have advanced the cause of materialism over spiritualism—with religion and family life in a state of decay. Instead of sticking together, family members each go off in their own direction today. When they do get together, they watch TV instead of communicating. Good books go unread. The media and entertainment industries believe that they must cater to low taste levels to be competitive. Quality in government has deteriorated, with an increasing lack of leadership and declining morality. Holding office has become an end justifying any means of getting elected. I see nothing but further decline in the offing—à la ''Rome'' of old—ending in some form of collapse. The possibility, finally, of a rejuvenation thereafter is obscured by the question of whether or not we will survive our own ingenuity at producing destructive weapons.

Operations executive (40 to 49), passenger railroad company, New York

While we are experiencing an ethical, moral, and spiritual decline in America, we are, at the same time, turning back, I believe, to more conservative national and religious principles. The signs of decline, however, are more apparent. The major factors contributing to this decline include (1) the failure of males to assume the real responsibilities of father in the home; (2) employment mobility and the separating of families from secondary relationships with grandparents, aunts, uncles, and cousins and their steadying influence; (3) the generally negative influence of the media (it is easy for people today to believe that the world is all bad and that everyone and every institution is corrupt); (4) our failure to censure the entertainment media for bringing bad language and sex right into our homes; (5) our affluence and increased leisure time that cause us to seek after lust and the so-called pleasures of life; and (6) the increased activ-

"The attitude that the world owes one a living does not foster reliance on one's own abilities and the need for Divine assistance."

ity of the powers of darkness (Satan and his angels). The only chance I see for a change for the better is hard times or a great turning back to God—and I do not want to see hard times.

Board chairman (40 to 49), wholesale grocery, Tennessee

I do support the contention that we are experiencing moral, ethical, and spiritual decay. Pick a topic—hunger, pollution, political and nonpolitical corruption, man's insatiable desire to dominate other men (skyrocketing defense budgets, Middle East wars, etc.), economic instability. I believe that these problems will continue to worsen as they have throughout history. The reason for this is that we simply have not learned to follow the Golden Rule in our dealings with one another as nations and as individuals. I believe that the ultimate result is going to be a world situation so corrupt and unbalanced that a great war ("Armageddon") must take place. Anyone who has followed historical trends cannot deny the strong possibility of this happening. What particularly saddens me is that I believe this great war will occur in *my* lifetime.

Controller (under 30), service laboratory, California

The moral, ethical, and spiritual fiber of this country has gone downhill fast. The major factors contributing to this decline include the laxity and permissiveness of a society that disregards the laws and demands of God. Witness the increase in drinking, drugs, tobacco, and pornography. Note the repeal of prohibition and the feeble attempts to control drug traffic. Look at the allowance of the use of tobacco even though proven to be a cause of cancer. Observe the Supreme Court rulings on sex-related matters. The Bible can no longer be read in public schools and X-rated movies are now shown on TV. Watergate certainly has made politics suspect. There will be no general improvement. Some people will buck the trend and remain true to

the Bible virtues. The only force that will eventually change this wicked world is the second coming of the Lord Jesus Christ.

President (50 to 59), engineering company, New York

I agree that we are in a moral, ethical, and spiritual decline. Several forces, in my opinion, have brought this about—one of the most important being a society of affluence which has allowed parents to provide for their children in terms of material goods and education while at the same time there is a lack of "togetherness" that has to a degree alienated the young.

Chief operating officer (50 to 59), insurance group, New Jersey

I believe that the social factors influencing moral and spiritual decline in America include liberal parental guidance (if any), the affluence of young people today, the rebellion of the young against social "norms" (good or bad), possibly women's "lib" and the "pill," the increasing use of alcohol and "dope" by both young and middle-aged people, and a lack of national direction and good governmental leadership. I believe that if inflation continues and if government and business cannot produce a stable system—financially and in terms of industrial growth—our country will continue to decline morally.

Engineering supervisor (50 to 59), New Jersey

The increasing affluence of our society, the development of the welfare state, the idea that the government is somehow required to guide and direct all of our activities, and the ever-increasing tax burden to pay for these programs leaves little incentive for personal improvement in our ethics and our moral and spiritual values. We have lost our self-reliance and tend to feel that somebody (the government) will provide for our needs, with little or no effort on our part. Unfortunately,

the decline in ethical, moral, and spiritual values in our society looks alarmingly like the fall of many ancient civilizations. When life becomes too easy, we feel no need for spiritual help from which come our moral and ethical attitudes.

Marketing director (50 to 59), packaging machinery company, Pennsylvania

I concur with the idea that we are experiencing a decline in ethical and moral behavior in America today. I feel very strongly that the breakdown in the family unit is a major cause of many of the ills that plague our society. Once the family unit disintegrates, chaos in our school system, greater public apathy toward government, and a general decline in social consciousness will take place. I feel, however, that the following measures would help to bring about a positive change: we need to better assist people in preparing for marriage, and we need to do more in preparing people for the conditions that follow separation or divorce.

Executive director (40 to 49), youth services agency, California

American society is definitely deteriorating due to ethical, moral, and spiritual paranoia. Many complex and intertwined forces have contributed to our national illness. At the risk of oversimplification, it is possible to isolate a few specifics. The root of the problem is the disappearance of the American frontier—geographically. The strongly individualistic approach to life that was encouraged by daily confrontation with the forces of nature has died out. In its place, we find the worst results of the Industrial Revolution—mass production of goods, people, ideas, values, and cultures. A worship of power and influence has replaced respect for individual contribution. The manipulation of people, individually and in groups, by a self-designated "elite," has become a way of life—politically, economically, and socially.

Americans have apparently forsaken the concept of individual liberty and responsibility. In its place, they seem to be asking for a monarchy or rigid feudal system, perhaps even a dictatorship, to limit the scope of their activities and minimize accountability. The "Renaissance man," daring to do many things well, has been replaced by the narrow "specialist" seeking personal security above all else.

Has this change been forced on Americans by the successive blows of the Depression of 1929, World War II, the atomic and space ages, and the short-lived "affluent society"? At the moment, this question is unresolved.

One factor, however, is identifiable. Inflation, resulting from human greed, has played an increasingly devastating role in American life. Beginning in the late fifties and early sixties with the rise of the credit card, inflation has warped the ideas, attitudes, and behavior of millions of Americans. The demand for more money, more creature comforts, more thrills, only generates dissatisfaction and disillusionment.

Symptomatic are the current quality of television programming, the prevalence of X-rated movies and pornography, the incidence of alcoholism and hard-drug addiction, the use of the contraceptive pill as an excuse for hedonism—"If it's fun, do it!"—and the resulting loss of meaning and purpose in life.

Many Americans, too many, have lost heart and initiative. They feel it is of no use even to attempt to reach their "level of incompetence." "What's the use?" "Why bother?" "Don't get involved!" These and related attitudes are expressed all too frequently. Until those many Americans learn to accept themselves as useful human beings, building on their strengths and doing their best to minimize their weaknesses, not much progress will be made.

There is a solution, a radical one. Some years ago in Chicago, Father

Robert Owens, a good Episcopal priest, worked as "Night Pastor" to the city. Until his untimely death, he met the demanding and unpredictable needs of the people all around him. His contribution was great, and his legacy even greater. Those who knew him or who have heard of him remember that he always wore a lapel button. The inscription? "Give a Damn!"

"WIN" buttons aren't doing too well. I'd like to see a resurgence of those earlier buttons. It could be the cure we need. "Give a Damn!"

Director of management operations (50 to 59), engineering company, Ohio

One contributing factor to moral, and spiritual decline in America has been the total lack of guilt experienced by the average person. Every day we see people force their way through traffic in their cars, with no feeling for the other guy or for whether it is legally and morally right to behave in this manner. We see workers doing two to three hours of work in a day and then complaining that they are overworked and underpaid. They don't feel guilty about this. People today cannot be objective about anything that affects them. To be objective would be to feel guilty. I see no change in the moral climate, especially since our leaders are the worst offenders.

Business division chief (30 to 39), public library, Maryland

I believe we are experiencing a moral, ethical, and spiritual decline—beginning, perhaps, during World War II. During the Great Depression, a frightened people clung to the church and looked to it for spiritual succor and moral guidance. Since then the influence of the church has suffered serious erosion, and nothing has replaced the church as a source of moral and ethical values. In my opinion, the shocking increase in crime, the Vietnam war with all its sordid revelations,

"We are bombarded today with every indication that sex is the paramount thing. We see this in advertising on TV and in all the short stories and modern novels that lead readers into thinking that this is the 'norm' in a good society."

and the actions of our political leaders as disclosed by Watergate will lead to a pulling back from the course we have been pursuing. A search will begin again for the values that once guided us. I firmly believe that the pendulum is swinging back the other way and that we are now at the beginning of a period of ethical, moral, and spiritual renewal.

Executive vice president (60 or over), insurance company, Minnesota

The press and media too must share responsibility for the decline in moral and spiritual values and behavior.

We are in the throes of a moral and ethical decline. I attribute a large part of the problem to radio, TV, and the free press. Communication is so rapid today—and coverage of events so complete—that our increased awareness is leading to a breakdown in our value systems. Unfortunately, the press and media tell us so much that is wrong with us because they think that is what we want to read and hear. I doubt that this trend can be stopped. But there is much that is good all around us. Hopefully the good will win out over the bad.

Organizational consultant (60 or over), certified public accounting firm, California

I support the contention that we are in the grip of an ethical, moral, and spiritual decline in American society.

TV, contemporary literature, and the news media—in that order of magnitude—have brought about this decay. I see no force that can bring us back to our former moral level. The only forces working for an improvement are our churches and the ethical committees in our various governmental bodies.

Technical vice president (50 to 59), paper company, South Carolina

Television and motion pictures are a big contributor to our national moral and ethical decline. I don't foresee a change for the better, but maybe tighter regulations could improve the situation.

Vice president, manufacturing (30 to 39), electronics company, California

Are we talking about the same thing when we talk about moral, ethical, and spiritual values or behavior? Some of us don't think so.

I'm not certain of the interdependence of ethical, moral, and spiritual values, but a spiritual decline is very obvious. However, this is not predicated on a decline in values or morals. In fact, I believe that the opposite is true.

Account executive (under 30), group insurance company, California

We must recognize that moral, ethical, and spiritual values are not equivalent—which is to say synonymous. For example, a car dealer who

closes up his shop on Sunday for religious motives may be unethical in some of his business practices. Similarly, a man who does not drink or smoke may be a child molester. I believe that our children must be taught that these three fundamental principles of human conduct are not, in fact, one and the same. Each must be cultivated, reinforced, and facilitated. In closing, it should be noted that both Goebbels and Stalin were reputed to be exemplary fathers.

Instructor (40 to 49), California university

On the brighter side, some of us feel that the moral and spiritual conditions in our society may not be as bad as many people think and that there are signs, moreover, that conditions are going to get better. Others question the assumption that morality is deteriorating and believe that the moral and spiritual climate in America is as good as or better than ever before. A few of us, finally, believe that changes in our ideas about moral and spiritual conduct need not imply something bad. In fact, quite the opposite may be true.

Ever since Adam bit the apple, people have had ethical, moral, and spiritual problems—and they still do. A review of history (take a look at the Roman Empire) will reveal that as a nation we are still a very respectable people. I foresee a change for the better as the Christian lay movement once again asserts itself and tells the clergy, "Follow if you will not lead." Remember, it was 12 disciples—all laymen—who changed the world for nearly 2,000 years, and not one had a degree in anything except love. I foresee the same in national affairs, as the "silent majority" crosses political boundaries and votes for the man and not the party. We will be saying in effect, "Only the best is good enough, because this is what my America was made of." The force that will eventually prompt this change is *us*. You and I and other millions of God-fearing, patriotic Americans who believe—not only in God and country—but also in ourselves.

Vice president and general manager (50 to 59), manufacturing company, Florida

I believe that society is slowly swinging back toward the older accepted moral standards. Civilization has a vast background of experience in what is necessary for people to live together. This experience will be brought to bear in subtle ways.

Chief engineer (40 to 49), environmental engineering company, New Jersey

I'm of an optimistic nature and foresee a change for the better in the moral, ethical, and spiritual climate. One of the main forces which could influence this change is that people in this country (and throughout the world) have seen so much injustice and corruption on the part of some leaders that they are searching for a renewal of a value system that is high in spiritual and ethical quality. I believe this is true of young people in addition to the middle-aged and the old.

Vice president and general counsel (60 or over), service company, Connecticut

Our ethical, moral, and spiritual decline is only real to a degree. Start a conversation on the subject and see how many people agree with the "decline" concept. Suffer a disaster and watch people respond. My area of the country was declared a disaster area in early 1974, and the most effective and capable 60 percent of the population responded immediately and with everything it had. I work with young people (ages 10 to 21) and see little deterioration and much resurgence in moral and spiritual strength. Our wars and booms, our liberal personal credit system, and easy living have helped to bring on the decline we *are* experiencing. The recession we are in will help to steady things. But it is the strong groundswell of spiritual development in our young people that will lift us out

of this slump. I would say that about 20 percent of our young people (ages 10 to 40) are absolutely without parallel in spiritual, moral, mental, and ethical strength. This country is just getting its feet on the ground.

Business manager (50 to 59), lumber products company, Washington

It is unfortunate that certain individuals who should know better allow themselves the luxury of claiming a lowering in our moral, ethical, and spiritual fund. Worse still, there is a tendency among so many people to dwell on the ''good old days.'' This mythology, while comforting, is neither realistic nor productive. In a technologically oriented society, we fail to see the neutrality of technique and the importance of human values. We fail to understand that values are that which provide direction. While technology has given us the A-bomb, it has also made us more aware of human needs and of how to satisfy them.

Assistant hospital director (40 to 49), university hospital, California

I don't agree that ethical, moral, and spiritual values in American society are declining. I believe that we have reached the bottom and that we are now in a period of rebuilding. The youth of America are our most important national resource. Through the 1960s and into the 1970s, our youth was without aim or purpose in life. However, I see an end to this life style and a rebirth of ethical, moral, and spiritual values among young people. We are exposed to all sorts of bad news concerning them. But I feel there are many good things being done by the young which we are not made aware of because good news doesn't make good news copy. The news media insist on reporting the worst things that happen because people, I guess, like to hear bad news. I feel that the next generation, however, will op-

erate from higher ethical, moral, and spiritual standards than people do today. America's hope is with its youth.

Personnel director (30 to 39), communications company, New York

I take issue with the contention that we are in an ethical, moral, and spiritual decline. I feel that human behavior has progressed gradually over the years in all three areas. If you study Biblical history, you will find evidence of this progress. Our progress, moreover, has been accompanied by technological advancement and a great improvement in the standard of living for large segments of the world's population. (We have had the atomic/hydrogen bomb for 30 years now and have not used it.) I believe that the climate will continue to improve as our educational processes improve. Our young people today are more inquisitive and more knowledgeable, and they will insist that these improvements be made.

Sales manager (40 to 49), metal products company, Connecticut

I don't believe we are in a moral, ethical, or spiritual decline. We have been living during a period of explosive expansion in communications, speed of travel, and reduced reaction time. We are much more aware today of the defects and problems all around us. Class barriers are fading away and our ''elite'' can no longer nurse illusions of noninvolvement with the rest of society. I see no change in our ethical ideals. I do see a greater awareness of the gaps between our ideals and our practices and less tolerance for hypocrisy. Our experience is a painful one, but probably for the better.

Research and development director (60 or over), multidivisional corporation, Ohio

I don't believe we are experiencing a moral decline. People have argued this from the beginning of time. There has been no appreciable erosion in our ethical, moral, and spiritual behavior in many centuries. If people would

"The influence of the church has suffered serious erosion, and nothing has replaced the church as a source of moral and ethical values."

spend less time worrying about the morality and fallibility of mankind and more time trying to bring about positive actions to correct our problems, the question wouldn't arise in the first place.

Vice president, secretary, and treasurer (30 to 39), professional service organization, Illinois

I am not so certain that we are experiencing so much of a decline in ethics, morals, and spiritual values as simply a change from past ideals and beliefs. Whether this is "right" or "wrong," a "decline" or an "upgrading" is for time to tell. I am certain in my belief, however, that the values and mores of a society must be open to change if that society is to survive. Those individuals, institutions, and societies that try to exist without accepting change soon cease to exist. Changes will come, and it is up to those in society who realize this to do whatever they can to guide those changes toward constructive ends. I do not advocate change simply for the sake of change, but as a way of working more effectively toward the accomplishment of goals.

Hospital administrator (under 30), Iowa

The many people who believe that America is in a state of moral and ethical decline are members of the older generation who refuse to accept the fact that all standards are (and must be) in a constant state of flux. Measurements are made on the basis of preconceived standards of behavior. While church attendance may be down, does that mean that we are less spiritual? Just because our sexual attitudes have changed, does that mean we are less moral? And who is qualified to pass judgment on ethics?

President (40 to 49), Louisiana company

Although more people than usual may be drifting today, I doubt that we are really experiencing a moral and spiritual decline. Indeed, the depth of spiritual and moral/ethical commitment is markedly stronger among many people today. This is especially true among younger people. Although values are changing, it is by no means clear that the change is negative in character. The extreme elements in society may be farther apart, but the "silent majority" is still there and stronger than ever. The freedom of expression that we see today covers a wider spectrum of opinion than it did in previous times, but this cannot be equated with moral, ethical, and spiritual decline.

Regional vice president (40 to 49), insurance company, California

"Scientific advances have advanced the cause of materialism over spiritualism—with religion and family life in a state of decay."

We want to talk briefly about some of the forces in our national life that we believe adversely affect the health and well-being of millions of Americans today—physically, emotionally, and psychologically. While some of us suspect that the negative impact of these forces is likely to intensify as time goes on, we are chiefly concerned with how these forces and the ill effects they produce affect our lives right now, today, and what we can do to check or reduce the damage they inflict.

The list of factors that we believe touch our daily lives in undesirable ways and contribute to personal feelings of frustration and anxiety is long. Included are urban overcrowding, advertising practices that distort our expectations and our sense of reality, the ''information explosion,'' current economic conditions and long-term economic mismanagement, modern communications and other aspects of advanced technology, the pace and character of change in virtually every area of our lives, and a kind of national compulsion to be first—number one—at everything.

SOCIAL TENSION

For sure, technology has to be the phenomenon which has had and continues to have a tremendous impact on the tension level in this country. Technology breeds intense competition. People have become vehicles of output—a "means to an end," so to speak. While we have been very industrially competitive domestically, the increase in international competition has only compounded the problem. We as a country need to reconsider the idea of being "number one" at any cost. We need to develop other, more appropriate values. The day may come when we are all acute neurotics on the verge of psychotic breakdowns. Look at the murder rate in this country. We are a rubber band about to break. We have got to reconsider the importance of being "number one" (competitive) at any cost.

Staff development director (under 30), U.S. government agency, Virginia

The constant pressure to remain a world leader has contributed substantially to increased tension in our lives. There is a gnawing fear today that as other countries aspire to a living standard similar to our own, there won't be enough to go around. We continually find the need to outproduce and outsmart the people of the world for fear of being overcome and overpowered by them. To reduce this tension, we should begin to live more and more like God-fearing people and to be not so afraid to share our resources with others. We should adopt an attitude toward other countries that is based on love, trust, and mutual respect—not on fear.

C.P.A. candidate (30 to 39), self-employed, Illinois

The major force in our national life most responsible for the increasing pressure associated with modern living is the speed and scope of mass communications, especially television. There was a time when it took months for news of major happenings to travel across the country. Today, we can witness news being made on the moon while it is happening. Man has not made himself ready to adapt to the increased pressure to assimilate, evaluate, and digest these events. Children can witness the slaughter of war as it happens thousands of miles away. Man, moreover, has further complicated his ability to cope by using the computer as more than just a simple tool. He has used it as a complex extension of himself.

Director of marketing and business development (under 30), information and research service company, New York

I believe that the constant bombardment of the public with television advertising in an effort to create mass demand has produced excessive dissatisfaction with reality and has led many to unrealistic expectations of rewards in exchange for modest efforts at best. We should limit the use of the media in this connection through taxation and other controls. This could decrease the feeling of dissatisfaction and help us restore normal human values. This might prevent a lot of social unrest and the subsequent pain and suffering that come from social upheaval.

EDP systems specialist (40 to 49), California

The tension-producing forces most affecting modern life are, in my opinion, related to government and politics. The lack of faith in Washington must be restored and the tremendous volume of unproductive paper work requirements must be limited. Too much is required in the way of paper work that produces nothing except an information file. Specifically, government agencies like the IRS, CAB, FTC, ICC, SEC, and others should limit their requirements on business. The trend toward more and more form-filing does indeed affect us today in our personal and business lives.

Controller (30 to 39), trucking company, North Carolina

"We're filling up our world with crowded cities and this results in internal friction and a vulnerable society."

Too many people live too close to-gether. Tension develops. We're filling up our world with crowded cities and this results in internal fric-tion and a vulnerable society. So much uninhabited land lies unused right here in the United States if we would only use it. Cities and private enterprise (not government) might benefit by funneling brainpower and other re-sources into developing incentives for new settlements in the West and Southwest. Surely science can do this here in our own backyard before it does it on the moon. In other words, a twenty-first-century pioneering spirit may just be the character-builder we need for the future.

Internal audit director
(30 to 39), chemical
company, Texas

Inflation and depression are the major causes of social tension today. Also, there is too much regulation by the government.

Financial analyst (30 to 39),
manufacturing company, Minnesota

One of my biggest concerns is the na-tional administration's clumsy ma-nipulation of the economy. Wage and price controls are the most recent extreme example. Continued deficit spending on the part of the government and the destructive taxing of individu-als and corporations are undermining our economic system, and the current insidious and pervasive inflation is corroding our national fabric. We need to reverse a long trend of wasteful ex-penditures of our national resources.

Staff executive (40 to 49),
capital equipment manufacturing
company, Washington

The main force in our national life most responsible for increasing social tension is the big desire for social status and social acceptance. Social gain is certainly a good objective, but to lessen its true meaning by using harsh means to attain it is not worthy of our "Americanism." We might be better off with less of a drive to achieve social status and more effort aimed at achieving mutual trust be-tween people.

Sales manager (40 to 49),
chemical producing
company, Pennsylvania

The greatest tension producer in our society is the information flow via communications, aided in some in-stances by the computer. With the in-formation explosion today, we have an overabundance of information at hand—an abundance that is often be-yond the individual's ability to absorb and put to good use. This creates ten-sion for sure. An ancillary fallout is the "invasion of privacy issue," which is an outgrowth of this ex-panded data flow.

Senior vice president
(40 to 49), automation equipment
company, New Jersey

Obviously there are a number of forces that work to increase the tension level in our society. They include (1) government—with its lack of sincere, intelligent leadership; corruption; greed, self-interest, and the feelings of futility they create; and deficit spend-ing which contributes to inflation; (2) mass media, which encourages or fos-ters delusions, unrealistic goals, overly optimistic expectations, moral decay, and a loss of family unity; (3) the population explosion, which has led to congestion, pollution (environ-mental destruction), and an indiffer-ence resulting in insecurity and fear; (4) advanced technology, which has given us—to our detriment—im-personalization, environmental pollu-tion, ease of convenience, and greater mobility (the transient nature of people today leads to a lack of meaningful friendships). To correct this situation people might begin to show more con-cern for others, might live from day to day rather than for the weekends only, and might try doing the best with what they have and start thinking positively for a change.

Corporate budgets manager
(30 to 39), real estate
development company, California

The tensions of modern life today are no doubt associated with a host of ills—some of which are exaggerated: (1) biased, pessimistic news reporting; (2) improved mass communications; (3) a widespread lack of religious and moral commitment (very few people today have "principles" or support "causes" that they would die for); and (4) most Americans are too willing to negotiate. It is apparent that the ills involved in the above are not easily eliminated and the social tensions that result are likely to continue. Most important, I believe we need to strengthen our religious and moral commitment and to improve our physical health and abilities as well. A "worn out" person has little inclination to worry, when sleep is so refreshing. In any event, I often feel that what is wrong with our society is grossly overstated. There are still those things in America that are good and beautiful and of good report.

Senior vice president, marketing
(40 to 49), Alabama bank

The one single item common to all men is the ability to resist change—or, in other words, the inability to accept it. While people say they want the "new" as it comes along, they don't really mean it. They want the same conditions to which they have become accustomed and with which they feel comfortable. They don't want to rock the boat.

Facilities manager (50 to 59),
Ohio corporation

The paramount force creating increased tension in modern society is the pace of change we are experiencing today. Technological advances since the end of World War II have been occurring at such a rapid pace in both the business world and in our private lives that we are faced with continual pressure to increase our knowledge of our surroundings. As a result, we have entered the "age of specialization" and must now defer so often to specialists to gain a sense of control over many situations. This produces frustration, and this frustration is likely to intensify, rather than subside, as improved technology in virtually all areas of human endeavor breeds more and more change. To better cope with this, we each need to look more closely into our own makeup and learn to accept our individual limitations and welcome new and challenging situations. We can ill afford to maintain the status quo or we will soon be bypassed.

Manager (40 to 49), oil field
equipment company, Texas

The increasing speed of change in all aspects of our lives—social, technological, political, etc.—has been mainly responsible for the increasing tensions associated with modern living. These tensions will continue to increase as long as education and communications lag behind the changes we are experiencing. It appears to me that we are already experiencing some changes in attitudes—especially among young people in our society—that prompt questioning and greater participation in all types of change. In our schools and in the business community, we need to develop programs to assist people in coping with change. We need to teach them how to keep up with what is going on and how to participate in the process of change rather than merely to accept change for change's sake.

Controller (50 to 59),
home products manufacturing
company, California

The forces most responsible for the increasing tensions and pressures in our lives today are those associated with the rapidity of change. The inability to adjust or to cope is a tension producer at a level of awareness difficult to work with. There's no question that this anxiety producer will continue to befuddle executives, workers, and families alike in an ever-increasing manner. Education in understanding the nature of change provides basic tools to minimize its impact on the human system. Courses in "change" might become part of corporate training programs. Another coping mechanism is man's search for community. There is a lasting quality in real interpersonal relating that provides a zone of stability that rides the wave of change. Increased emphasis on providing gathering places and a proper climate for relating meaningfully might be a step in a helpful direction. *Professor (50 to 59), California university school of business*

Historically, mankind has found it very difficult to adapt to rapid change. Our nation in its development has created for our people a changing environment never before experienced by mankind. The present interest being shown by many of our citizens in objects, customs, music, etc., that are part of a past age indicates to me that people are seeking to slow—or even reverse—the clock. How do we reduce these tensions? One way is for individuals to find something to cling to that does not change rapidly. The Christian religion is the best thing of that kind that I know of—and I am not a religious nut. I believe that we must shed, to some degree, our selfishness and adopt, to a greater degree, the belief that we are our brother's keeper. *Board chairman (50 to 59), holding company, Tennessee*

The director of employee training and development for an Alabama firm is concerned about the extent to which government and big business manipulate events at the expense of the little fellow. A village administrator from Illinois writes about the growing restrictions on some of our freedoms—including the "freedom to fail." And a manager from Wisconsin believes that statistical half-truths, vacillating standards of measurement, and abnormality-dominated news media are principal among the factors that create problems for many Americans today.

For almost 20 years I have had close continuing contact with college students across the United States. I am convinced that for many years the Vietnam war coupled with compulsory military service was the most upsetting force responsible for increasing tensions among college-age people and their parents. Fortunately, this pressure has been removed. We have also unquestionably experienced a deterioration in our moral and spiritual values. This is evidenced by more liberal divorce laws and court rulings on such issues as Bible reading and prayer in public schools. On the latter issue, we have penalized the majority in order to please a small minority, and this runs counter to the basic democratic principle of majority rule. Further, American industry has betrayed the American consumer. We have all come to expect a certain amount of exaggeration in advertising, but quality products at a reasonable price are hard to find. Many of the "standard brand" items have become absolutely unreliable in recent years. Large American corporations (from oil companies to sugar processors) have manipulated the market so completely that the consumer has literally become their "victim." At the same time, it is a nationally known fact that these corporations are increasing their profits at unbelievable rates.

Our central government itself has contributed in many ways to this gross abuse of the American consumer. For example, government controls on agricultural products (such as cotton, wheat, and soybeans) were removed in 1974. Farmers were urged to plant all they could because there was a world shortage of food and a world market therefore for all that America's farmers could produce. Look what followed: By late summer of 1974 grave predictions were made by government economists (prodded by industrial lobbyists) that the U.S. food surplus was dangerously low and that the sale of grain and other food and fiber products to countries like Red China and Russia would cause a major crisis in the United States. The president responded by imposing an embargo in the early fall of 1974—just as the harvest was getting under way. The result was that farm prices including beef took a nose dive. Farmers had sold their annual crop for less than half the price level by mid-summer. Just as the harvest was essentially over, the president lifted the embargo. Now guess where the farmers' products were by then? They were in the hands of the speculators—the ''middlemen,'' whose only interest in the grain market is in making a profit. Immediately, ships were loaded at Memphis, New Orleans, and other ports for shipment to foreign countries—like China and Russia—which had caused our government officials so much concern during the summer.

Farmers are no longer ignorant of such manipulating. They are educated and sophisticated enough to understand what has happened and why it happened. As a result, independent farm groups are banding together to market their own products. They are beginning to butcher, process, and market their own beef in Iowa, Tennessee, and other states. Bigness in corporations is not an evil in itself. But large corporations must develop a public conscience and adhere to integrity in their business practices.

Director of employee training and development (50 to 59), aerospace research company, Alabama

One of society's greatest problems involves trying to protect incompetent people from harm by imposing restrictions on everyone else. We are losing our freedom because of this misguided philosophy. We are losing the freedom to fail, the freedom to take chances with our lives, even the free-

dom to drive a car without wearing seatbelts. We need the opportunity to do as we damn please just so long as others are not put in jeopardy by our actions. Also, our courts and civil libertarians are removing discipline from our society and creating a serious lack of observance of the law and the rights of the law-abiding citizens of our nation.

Village administrator (50 to 59), Illinois

Oversimplification and Prince Machiavelli have given amnesty to leadership in America. The featured culprit is always the government at all levels. But it is the educational system that has sidetracked philosophy in favor of argumentation; the press, selling abnormality for news (''man bites dog'' is a basic theme); business and advertising, packaging materialism as sure-fire success; abusing statistical evidence (Carl Jung told us 20 years ago that this abuse would be the downfall of the Western world); intelligence measured by cunning rather than wisdom (e.g., Grossman's *The Change Agent*). The end does not justify the means. Common sense, without formal education, recognizes that ''disease'' is more contagious than ''health.'' False premises, improper objectives, vascillating standards of measurement, statistical half-truths, and an abnormality-dominated media have gotten us into the condition we're in today.

Manager (50 to 59), Wisconsin company

"Man has further complicated his ability to cope by using the computer as more than just a simple tool. He has used it as a complex extension of himself."

Finally, some of us believe that intense competition, a growing dependency on others, not knowing how to deal with new or unfamiliar situations, and the failure of the dollar-oriented ethic to provide a satisfying life contribute in major ways to the tension, pressure, and anxiety that so many people experience in their daily lives.

Today's pressures are the result of the fast pace of things, caused by intense competition, the "atomic age," and the electronic media. These tensions will continue to intensify in the future. Meditation is effective in reducing tension. Self-esteem, self-worth, and a sense of identity must be reestablished through programs such as transactional analysis. Job enrichment must be fostered through "team" concepts. If we adopt an attitude that embraces change, growth, and learning, we will not only be able to better cope with but will actually enjoy our work and lives.

Sales manager (50 to 59), capital equipment manufacturing company, Massachusetts

In our modern industrial society, people are no longer able to be self-sufficient. The vast majority of our population will not be able to exist if the system breaks down. Yet we have concentrated on becoming "economic man," without sufficient awareness of the needs of all mankind. We are deluded into pursuing the wrong goals. We are frustrated by our inability to provide solutions for the real problems of our world—war, hunger, etc. We must widen our horizons.

General manager (50 to 59), home products manufacturing company, Indiana

The increased tensions and pressures in our society are the direct result of people trying to change as new information and technology become available at an ever-increasing rate. To try to keep pace with all the new developments in the marketplace is really tough, from a technical point of view. I can see where there is a need for more and more "specialization" in order to keep pace. Tension and pressure are created by our not knowing how to handle a particular situation. A good manager today must accept the attitude that he or she doesn't have all the answers. Tomorrow's manager will have to have the ability to call upon various specialists to assist in the decision-making process. Management today makes many decisions based on intuition, past experience, and "seat of the pants" methods. This type of management approach cannot be regarded as maximally effective.

Executive, retail stores (30 to 39), multidivisional corporation, California

The structure of our society is changing because of the failure of the dollar-oriented ethic to provide a satisfying life and due to the passing of the worship of technology. The redistribution of the world's power and wealth will force us, the most consuming society in all of history, to adjust our levels of living. We will eventually learn to do more with less and will, I believe, enjoy life more as a result. The pain of this change will be proportional to the degree that we believe the change to be unnecessary.

District sales manager (40 to 49), Pennsylvania company

"We will eventually learn to do more with less and will, I believe, enjoy life more as a result. The pain of this change will be proportional to the degree that we believe the change to be unnecessary."

The investment we make in education is one of the largest we make in the United States today. While some of us believe that this investment is paying off—that the American educational system is the very best in the world and that substantial reform is unnecessary—others insist that the process *is* in need of complete, or significant, overhaul.

In this chapter we want to talk about *what* we teach our young people today and the *way* in which we teach them. Are we adequately preparing our nation's youth to deal with the realities of human experience? Are we preparing them to cope successfully with the present and future challenges they are likely to face? Some of us think that we are doing this, or that we are certainly doing a better job in that respect than ever before. But others tend to disagree, are not so certain, or are convinced that the educational system in America today is failing in many ways to prepare young people to earn a living and to live satisfying lives.

EDUCATION

"There is, in my opinion, entirely too much amateurish switching of techniques in our learning institutions today. Every year, new methods are introduced, based on fads or shallow hypotheses."

I think that what we teach and the way we teach young people today can stand vast improvement. However, I don't believe that a complete overhaul of our educational system is the answer. There are too many questions that lack sufficient answers to warrant such sweeping change. Instead, we must learn through experiment and theoretical analysis how to develop meaningful methods that will lead to improved teaching techniques. There is, in my opinion, entirely too much amateurish switching of techniques in our learning institutions today. Every year, new methods are introduced, based on fads or shallow hypotheses. As a result, some older yet better techniques are discarded. Often, when new methods fail, other, even less proven ideas, are introduced.

Manager (50 to 59), industrial research laboratory, Pennsylvania

Complete overhauls, though frequently suggested, are seldom needed. Today's educational system and processes have been propelled by innovations in recent years into unproven and in some instances counterproductive areas. Specifically, the innovations of the past have resulted in a failure to accomplish true learning of the 3 R's. Another shortcoming has been the failure to instill a quest for knowledge, due to the emphasis on "relevance of education." The realities of life can only be successfully dealt with by mentally, physically, and spiritually

healthy people motivated to work for continued and continuous self-improvement. We can accomplish this objective with systematic changes short of complete overhaul.

Educator (40 to 49), state university, Pennsylvania

I believe that our public educational system is the best in the world at the present time, despite its many weaknesses. The trend toward individualization in instruction that began in the 1960s and the encouragement of innovative course design and instruction is excellent. Unfortunately, many school districts have discontinued funding of these projects after withdrawal of federal support. Another promising note is the realization by school administrators, counselors, and parents that everyone does not need a college education to succeed and to find satisfaction in life. Our children, however, are being better prepared for life today than we were.

Executive (40 to 49), instructional materials design and development company, Pennsylvania

Today's educational goals do not account for change, and they are static. Our youth should be taught about the process of birth, growth, and death—about change. They should be better taught how to decide things for themselves and how to commit themselves to life.

Administrative social worker (30 to 39), state government, New Jersey

I strongly believe our educational system needs to be overhauled. We need to pay male instructors better salaries to get them to remain in teaching jobs at the elementary level. We need to develop better educational methods for slow learners—"gifted" students will make it. We need to encourage more trade and technical skills training—a literary education is not for everyone. I endorse the idea of greater community involvement—but not community con-

trol. We need to encourage better parent/school relationships. We need to provide more and better extracurricular activities to keep otherwise alienated—or potentially alienated—students in school. And, finally, we need teachers and administrators who care more about young people.

Program director (30 to 39), government outreach program, District of Columbia

I agree that we need a complete overhaul of our educational system and process. What we are teaching and the way we are teaching have not changed decidedly since the 1920s. There is still too much "rote" learning and memory work in what educators and laymen call "college preparatory work." Hence, too many of our college graduates leave school with an accumulation of college credits in "copied" term papers and memorization. They major in subjects where they merely receive a textbook education—or a "regurgitation education" from college professors. Students who do not go on to college are left to fend for themselves. We need to restructure our educational system for the college-bound as well as the noncollege-bound.

Personnel development manager (40 to 49), group broadcasting company, Florida

I have grave concern for the teaching methods and subject matter being taught in primary and secondary schools today. The impact of TV and "progressive education" has produced young people with impressive vocabularies, narrow interest areas, and a low level of understanding in most subjects. In view of the changing social environment, the next generation will no doubt speed the trend toward the new work ethic and push productivity even lower. These people need revitalized educational programs now!

Vice president (30 to 39), manufacturing company, Florida

Yes, we do need a basic overhaul of our educational system. We should provide our young people a chance at an earlier age to choose the educational path they want to follow based on their aptitudes. We should be better preparing young people to earn a living at the time they graduate from high school. Our school system is too oriented toward producing scholars rather than men and women who can be functional citizens. I am not qualified to comment on teaching methods, but I back the idea of innovation in teaching approaches. I definitely feel that we do not adequately prepare our young people to deal with the realities of life.

Executive (40 to 49), natural gas distribution company, Michigan

Most of what is taught at the elementary, high school, and college levels is sufficient and appropriate. However, some educators utilize "mod" literature because of its shock value when, in fact, it has no redeeming literary attributes. Otherwise, the quality of the curriculum in our schools is good. Generally, teaching methods are also good. College teachers are seldom selected, of course, for teaching ability, and many work only a few hours a week at teaching. This situation should be improved and teachers should find out more about the world of work. Young people today receive very little personal assessment and career guidance at the high school level and little more in most colleges. Campus employment recruiting results in astronomical turnover rates. Liberal arts and education majors don't know what to do with themselves in seeking employment. Most vocational guidance counselors are well intentioned but don't know anything to speak of about employment prerequisites, candidate evaluation, and job opportunities. (New computer techniques may help to bridge this gap in the education-employment process.) Some college schemes designed to

force 17-year-old men and women into living too closely together in dormitories seem to have been ill conceived and poorly executed. Only the inherent common sense of the kids has saved them from emotional difficulties. Effective preparation for dealing with the realities of human experience should also require educating our young people about our American capitalistic system, what profit is, where it comes from, and how it is used.

Personnel manager (40 to 49), electrical wholesale company, Connecticut

There is no question in my mind but that our educational process needs an overhaul. A good percentage of today's youth who do not complete college are not otherwise properly prepared to be productive, wage-earning citizens. Nearly 80 percent of our high school graduates have taken a college prep course, yet only 25 percent of these students actually graduate from college. The balance do not have marketable skills that enable them to successfully enter the job market. With over 20,000 career possibilities in the United States, it should be possible through career counseling to start students on the road to a satisfactory and enjoyable career long before high school graduation. In addition to contributing to the unemployment ranks, our outdated educational system is also costing the taxpayers—and business —28 billion dollars annually. I firmly believe that the future of American business and the free market system is tied to our educational process. This process must be amended to provide vocational and career skills training through the high school level.

Personnel manager (30 to 39), multinational corporation, Ohio

The schools in my community are not only failing to educate our youth, but too frequently they develop in young people an aversion to learning. The schools here have not changed tech-

"The impact of TV and 'progressive education' has produced young people with impressive vocabularies, narrow interest areas, and a low level of understanding in most subjects."

niques in over 50 years. It is not only the "drop-out" that points to the system's failure, but the average graduate with no understanding of economics, no vocational guidance, and no real assistance in deciding whether he or she should go on to college, trade school, or into an apprenticeship. The typical student has not learned how to think—how to distinguish fact from fantasy. The whole educational system needs revision, starting with the selection of teachers who are sensitive to our youngsters—teachers trained in human relations. We need to pay more attention to the selection and training of principals, and we need to make a better selection of subject matter so as to better prepare youngsters for thinking and for life. We need to take power away from the teachers' unions so that teachers can be evaluated on the basis of competency and rewarded for innovation. We need to give students and parents a greater voice in the decision-making process in our schools. Until drastic changes are made, only bright, highly motivated students will graduate with a decent education—and this will be in spite of, not because of, our present educational system.

Payroll and accounting manager (40 to 49), manufacturing company, Illinois

While an executive from Missouri thinks that what we teach is much more realistic than what was taught in the past, many of us believe there's plenty of room for improvement in teaching methods and curricula in our educational system today.

It seems to me that what we teach our children today is much more realistic than what was taught before the last decade or so. We seem to be willing now to face up to the facts of life and to recognize that young people in school must face these problems too and that we should not only help to define them, but provide guidance by suggesting alternative solutions for students to consider. We also need to help students to learn to take advantage of their individuality in a rather complex world. Likewise, the way in which we teach children seems to me to be much better than in past years. Children today are given much more individual attention—at least in the public schools and colleges with which I am familiar. In this way, the educational program is molded to the child or young person rather than the person being made to fit into an educational mold not necessarily designed for him. These teaching methods, in a complex society, contribute to improved individual interest in learning and produce more knowledgeable students.

As to whether or not we are adequately preparing today's youth to deal with the realities of human experience—that's an open question. We certainly do not prepare every individual to deal with these realities, but we do offer enough variety in educational programs and do pay more personal attention to the individual. I have two daughters who are currently teaching senior high school students, and through them I have been able to keep somewhat up to date on teaching methods. Much progress has been made. I also serve on the board of a

large four-year college and never cease to marvel at the innovative programs being implemented at the college level.

Senior vice president (60 or over), insurance company, Missouri

During the last 20 years, our educational system has moved from one end of the discipline spectrum (formal) to the other—to little or no academic self-control. This situation has generated a selfishness within the business community which can no longer be tolerated if we are to overcome the rigors of our current economic slowdown. We have lost the ability and the desire to roll up our sleeves and get to work by neglecting to inculcate students with sound values. Our academic institutions have led a generation to revolution in the name of impractical social utopian ideals. The educational system must get back to the middle ground and reinstitute reasonable disciplines.

Financial officer (40 to 49), New York bank

The educational system in the United States does not generally prepare America's youth to cope with socioeconomic reality today. The educational institution and many teaching methods are—with some exceptions—the same as they were 30 years ago. Too much emphasis is placed today on theory and not enough on sound creative thinking as it relates to the real world. Qualifications to serve on school boards are lax, PTAs are ineffective, and the tenure system

should be abolished throughout the teaching profession. Educators today are teaching mechanically about a world they know very little about—and what is worse is the apparent public apathy.

Personnel director (30 to 39), consumer finance and insurance company, Indiana

While I am not in possession of sufficient factual information to conclude that our public education system requires complete overhaul, I do believe that the system needs a basic reevaluation. Adequately preparing today's youth to effectively deal with the realities of human experience is a rather dubious objective. The educational system should direct its resources to the attainment of a standard of excellence rather than mere adequacy.

Corporate counsel (30 to 39), consulting company, Florida

We are not adequately preparing our youth to effectively deal with reality at present. Too much emphasis is placed on the attainment of the highest grades or on what a degree will mean in the labor market. This emphasis is misplaced. We don't emphasize what one can contribute, but the easy methods of skirting hard work and getting away with it. It is man's privilege as well as his obligation to work. It is a divine gift, if you will, to master the forces of nature, to improve the environment, to be creative. Only in these endeavors does man rise above other creatures. Children, young people, and all people everywhere need to again be taught that the world cannot progress on mere theories and abstract principles—no matter how idealistic.

Employee of nonprofit national organization (60 or over), New York

Schools have become all wrapped up in the process of being schools and have forgotten the importance of guiding young minds through a meaningful learning experience. Rules and procedures for the convenience of teachers limit potentials. A more complete education would be possible for our young people if teachers and educators would look more to the world outside the classroom for experiences to enrich the minds of the young by relating the real world to the textbook.

Marketing and sales director (40 to 49), manufacturing company, Mississippi

Some subjects taught today are not very useful, practical, or applicable. These courses are holdovers from the past. They should be available for interested students, and their possible utility should be explained to everyone. However, required subjects should be clearly useful to students, and parents and teachers have a responsibility to guide students in this regard. Educational methods must be modern and competitive with other forms of education that the young person acquires on his or her own, through associations with others, or through the media bombardment we are all exposed to every day. We must exert more effort in teaching every student to be responsible and how to differentiate between following the crowd and being an individual. Very importantly, students need to be taught where to get the help needed to help them make that decision.

Educational administrator (40 to 49), private hospital, Wisconsin

I believe that our educational system at all levels—elementary school, high school, and college—has disintegrated during the past few decades and no longer provides the individual a solid intellectual base with which to make sound judgments affecting his everyday life. The new generation has not been taught the basics in terms of the social, economic, and political ideas inherent in a democracy. Consequently, our work ethics, social programs, and moral attitudes have been adversely affected.

Plant manager (40 to 49), manufacturing company, California

Our educational system is not adequately preparing children to deal with the realities of human experience. It is preparing all of them for a college education rather than directing them toward useful occupations in line with their capabilities. I believe that everyone is entitled to a college education, but I don't believe that everyone *should* be in college. The process is unfair, sets unrealistic goals, and places too much importance on levels of achievement. Students should be made aware that a career as an auto mechanic can be much more rewarding than the experience of a person with a Ph.D. in education who has reached a high level of achievement and is unhappy.

Technical director (40 to 49), hospital, New York

Perhaps the single most important factor that is missing from education today is that of teaching the student that he is not only a responsible person but that he will and must be held accountable for the decisions he makes and the actions he takes. Most educational programs preach the development of a "value system," but the evidence is overwhelming that people turn out to usually hold others—not themselves—responsible for things. Situation ethics which dominate our educational system are affecting everything we do, and they do not work.

Director of university computing (30 to 39), Indiana

"Children, young people, and all people everywhere need to again be taught that the world cannot progress on mere theories and abstract principles—no matter how idealistic."

As an active professional educational administrator for the past 30 years, I believe that public education is clearly involved in a complete overhaul engineered by educators, special interest groups, and our court systems. I believe that a very significant and effective partnership between education, business and labor, and our federal and state governments is emerging. This partnership will clearly improve the quality, efficiency, and the product of our very large investment in public education. Through extensive research, content and method are both being modified to meet the demands of this new partnership. This partnership, I believe, will better equip our children, youth, and adults to deal effectively with the realities of both today and tomorrow.

District superintendent (50 to 59), public school system, California

The role of the educator—both in the classroom and outside—is critical to quality education, in our view.

Our educational system does need overhauling. My profession has not provided the kind of leadership that is needed. As a result, what we teach and the way we teach fall short of what we have a right to expect from our schools. All of this will improve only to the extent that standards of quality and quantity are imposed from outside the teaching profession. I sense that a private, independent effort is in the making within the educational institution to do its share through an all-out commitment to improving education.

President (60 or over),
Michigan college

What we teach our youth and the way we teach them are intertwined. So much more is learned because of the teacher's attitude that we need to pay more attention to such things as the "openness" or "closedness" of teachers. To what extent do some instructors teach merely to satisfy a power need? Does school administration add to or detract from the teaching/learning process? The "lockstep" concept must be abandoned and a high degree of testing proficiency and individualization in instruction must be pursued.

Director (30 to 39), continuing
education program, Virginia

To me, what and how we teach seem to be controlled today by unknown and "far-out" educators. The approach most teachers use is based on statistics and facts, as if they were dealing with computers rather than human beings who should learn how to use their logic and reasoning abilities. Teachers don't seem to take much pride in accomplishment. Teaching has become an "8 to 5 and let's get out of here" profession.

Analyst (40 to 49), EDP
systems and programming
company, Kansas

I believe that young people (adolescents and young adults) today are basically and naturally too intelligent for our educational system. The courses offered, the teaching methods, and the teachers themselves should be closely analyzed. Teachers should be required to work in industry for at least three years prior to receiving their teaching credentials. Students should receive a broad introduction to careers and the best way to prepare for them at a very early age—around the eighth grade. Also, students should be taught the art of self-motivation and autosuggestion beginning at the third-grade level and continuing through high school. Parents should be required to attend classes in human relations and in how to cope with everyday problems and challenges.

Student recruitment manager
(30 to 39), technical
institute, Illinois

*S*ome of us agree that we need to do more to gear the educational process to better serve the unique needs of each student.

Some schools are trying to humanize their programs and do away with the authoritarian structure that most adults are familiar with from their own educational experience. We need to think of each student as a person—entirely different from any other person—and provide him with teachers and a learning environment that will best enable him to learn in the most effective manner. Today's institutions can stifle the individual and impede his progress.

*Assistant superintendent
(40 to 49), public school
district, Ohio*

I believe that much improvement can be made in the way we teach our children. It seems that machine teaching will be less emotional, more factual and uniform, providing more opportunity for pupil "repeat-back." This new method should allow for better concentration, less distraction, and more individual attention being given each individual student.

*President (40 to 49), engineering
company, Indiana*

In my opinion, we have made an error in the idea that all students must be educated in the same way, the same manner, and the same place. All students should receive training in the basics—in reading and writing, in being good citizens, in economics and the economic system, in money management, in buying a home or a car.

Students should be trained on an individual basis in how to make a living—in the arts and crafts and trades for those who are so inclined. Higher education should be reserved only for those with the IQ, aptitude, and desire that college training requires.

*Executive (60 or over),
science and electronics
company, California*

"Overhaul" implies massive change, and I believe that's an impossibility. Systematic change, on the other hand, is vitally needed. Today, we "train" students rather than "educate" them. Our educational system is geared to the "average"—whatever that is! It doesn't serve the individual needs of each student. We kill the gifted, dampen the desire of the above-average, patronize the average, and smother the below-average. We claim that education is a right, that education is for the student—what hypocrisy! If education is for the student, then why is all the power in the hands of teachers and administrators? Students need to be given some of that power too. Most educational systems are publicly operated, which I believe hampers their ability to innovate and make changes. Perhaps a system based on private initiative with public funding should be tried.

*Director (30 to 39),
Minnesota association*

99

Some of us are concerned with how much emphasis should be placed on early specialization and vocational training. One of us believes that students should work for a year or so following high school, before going on to college.

With all the increasing concern over improving the "quality of life," we find the curricula at both the high school and college levels emphasizing vocational education (including courses in business management) while eliminating courses in the humanities. It appears that educators have either misinterpreted the future needs of the nation's youth or they simply find it easier to teach students accounting than to guide them to an appreciation of English literature. This trend will lead to a nation of "fat bellies" and Bowmar brains. If we are going to concern ourselves with the quality of life, why not teach our children how to recognize it?

Financial analyst (under 30),
Ohio hospital

We are not adequately preparing youth to deal with the realities of human experience. The many years of educational preparation keep students in school much too long. I favor reducing the number of years spent in precollege education. Perhaps students should do something else for a year or so after high school. Then they would return to school more highly motivated and glad to be back again. They might

be more grateful for the opportunity to learn and more anxious to prepare themselves for useful careers. I believe that our school system should stress more than it does the ability to read, to quantify, and to reason. Enrichment is fine, but it should not take the place of class time for serious study.

Dean and professor (50 to 59),
Rhode Island university

I agree that our educational system needs a complete overhauling. Before we can accomplish this, however, we have a long-range problem to overcome: that of getting people to set more realistic goals for themselves and for the nation as a whole. Until recent years, the vast majority of our young people aimed at achieving a significant education and at getting a good position in the economy. When it became apparent that not every American child could or should go to college, some attempts were made to provide better vocational training as an alternative. Unfortunately, this effort was a failure because most young people viewed vocational work as a stigma implying stupidity. The next innovation on the part of schools was to become very permissive and to create endless

causes that lacked significant content and apparent value. As a result, education in many places has become meaningless and the drop-out rate has increased.

Ultimately, in my opinion, we must install an educational system modeled after those in Western Europe, where the privilege of a university education is reserved for those who qualify from an academic and intellectual standpoint. All other students would be offered the opportunity—and be required—to participate in meaningful, modernized, advanced vocational training which would qualify them to move immediately into the vocational area of their choice.

Consultant (60 or over),
brewing company, California

One of the most serious mistakes made in mass public education has been the early and persistent stress on "specialization"—from elementary school right up through college. Men and nations would be much better served if people were afforded an education in how to *think*. That kind of an education would better prepare them for the five to seven roles they will likely be called on to assume during adult life to provide for their own and their family's well-being.

Chief administrator
(30 to 39), public historical
agency, Illinois

I believe we need a change in our high schools away from a heavy emphasis on liberal arts or college prep programs and toward a more comprehensive vocational training program. We need to encourage more "hands on" experience for students and less textbook work. And all teachers should make a point of visiting the business community periodically to find out what's going on.

Business manager (50 to 59),
public school, Wisconsin

What can we legitimately expect from our educational system today? How do other factors in the community at large affect what we teach our young people and the way in which we teach them? Are there valuable educational resources in our communities that we are failing to take advantage of?

"Too many of our college graduates leave school with an accumulation of college credits in 'copied' term papers and memorization."

Adequate preparation for the realities of human experience is attained by living the human experience to the fullest with due consideration for other human beings. Education has too long been utilized as the whipping boy for deficiencies in family obligations and personal initiative. Current school systems, for the most part, are attempting to teach children more at an earlier age and in a more enlightened atmosphere. If some people doubt the knowledgeability of children, perhaps they are not spending enough time talking with them. Talking with a child is an enlightenment that enhances our own human experience. If we expect children to be ready for tomorrow, we must participate with them today and allow them to participate with us.

Manager (30 to 39), moving and storage company, Illinois

Much of the discussion concerning the educational system—including the criticism—has been geared to the "what we are teaching" and the "way we are teaching it" in our schools. Practically no notice has been taken of the fact that society's demands on education have been in a state of continual change, particularly during the past two decades. The question is not only "can we prepare today's youth to deal effectively with living in a period of change?"—the variables of which cannot be forecast with any accuracy—but also "what does society actually expect from the schools?" Schools have moved a long way from teaching the 3 R's, and presently there is no consensus as to what society's goals for schools really are or should

be. Schools today transport, feed, and babysit students, handle societal discipline problems, provide psychological and sociological assistance, deal in health and social problems—including adult-instigated vices such as drug abuse, alcohol, and smoking—and are active in every conceivable area of human adjustment. When society decides what the role of the school is to be in today's environment, then schools will meet the challenge by gearing themselves to accomplishing these goals.

Superintendent of schools (50 to 59), Wisconsin school district

What we teach children has little relationship to what they will need to cope with society and their existence in it. There are a lot of false ideas about education today. One false notion is the intrinsic or implied premise that educational attainment is a "magic carpet" to success in life. Another is the simplistic idea readily promoted by the educational system itself that there are, in fact, implementable solutions to all problems—particularly social ones. Finally, we have witnessed a proliferation of educational techniques and "fads" that guarantee knowledge with little or no effort. Witness the penchant today for talking ("rapping," it is called) about problems rather than addressing ourselves to their solution.

Assistant director (30 to 39), state agency, Texas

Our schools are caught in the goals overload dilemma of providing more and more social and psychological services (based on parental expectations) in addition to providing basic academic skills. Within this situational setting, factors (home and family life and other social forces in society) beyond the control of the educational system continuously act as counter-influences on the efforts of school professionals. A reorientation of education should focus on a curriculum for survival competencies—the basics or fundamental academic and social skills (career education), on increased support services in counseling, on increased job autonomy for teachers, and on a variety of work-study program alternatives for students.

Professor of education (50 to 59),
state university, Missouri

In contrast to much of the publicized opinion concerning our educational system, I feel that the schools have certainly set their goals correctly and are driving toward them. The rigidity of subject matter has lessened. Individualized teaching programs are in working order. Outside resource people from industry, government, and the professions are being used extensively. In my experience both higher educational institutions and high schools are career-oriented for the most part. The store of knowledge is gaining on us too fast for any school to be able to teach students what they will actually use. Wisely, they are orienting themselves toward teaching students how to assimilate and apply knowledge. Of course, there is a room for improvement, but certainly our schools are aware and caring. Young people who want to be will be equipped to deal with any problems that occur.

Director of industrial relations
(50 to 59), oil and natural
gas company, Texas

The problem that critics of education do not recognize is that schools are subject to all the pressures and forces in society at large. Crime, minority

demands, resistance to authority, dwindling resources, labor-management disputes—all of these factors affect the educational process. The notion that school management is free to unilaterally change the system is so naive as to border on stupidity. All of the problems implied in your question do exist in the communities in which schools must function. When these problems are resolved by the larger community, they can be solved in the schools.

Assistant superintendent (40 to 49),
city school district, Michigan

Education! A galloping bureaucracy, uncontrolled, untouchable, and in drastic need of change. Talk about a syndicate! Corrective measures and curricula changes can only take place when we find a solution to disinterest on the part of a majority of the residents living within each individual school district.

Purchasing director (40 to 49),
New York bank

Our educational system has been overhauled and is in a constant state of change. Nevertheless, because education is largely a matter of local control, many inconsistencies are apparent depending on local socioeconomic conditions. The "what" and the "way" we teach our children are also inconsistent. I see no hope for changes nationally, but new processes and methods are making inroads where local climates allow. To better equip our young

people to handle the realities of human experience, many communities have introduced courses in drug abuse, sex education, and family planning. These courses can be very helpful in preparing young people for adult life. Few such programs existed ten years or so ago, and, while available today, they are not available in all of our school systems because of local thinking.

Personnel director (40 to 49),
Connecticut company

An overhaul of the educational institution and processes is not needed. But we do need to improve the processes now utilized and to revitalize the institutional means of implementing them. To the extent that all Americans realize that there is a fundamental difference between schooling (which is institutionalized) and education (which is a lifelong process), we can improve both schooling and education. I find more and more earnest efforts being made to interface schooling with other societal institutions in ways which are beneficial to the whole community. Involvement of corporations, commercial enterprises, military organizations, religious organizations, and others with schools and universities can (if we have the will) result in improvement of our schools and benefit not only young people but all the members of our society.

Superintendent (40 to 49), county
public school system, Florida

There is a vast reservoir of retired people from business, the military, etc., able and willing, but not asked by our educators, to provide assistance and guidance in evaluating our educational system today. Who is better prepared to counsel our students and educators—people who have experienced the world of business or the educator and his textbooks?

Personnel manager (60 or over), public utility, Maryland

"Complete overhaul" may be too severe a description for what I feel is needed—and missing—in our educational system today. The business community and the American way of producing goods through the capitalistic system of free enterprise are being attacked by teachers in college today, and business has reached a new low in popularity among college students. Qualified businessmen should be given sabbaticals to teach at colleges and universities, so that students at least get a chance to hear the business side of the story. I believe the result will be increased productivity and an increased ability on the part of business to attract top-grade students.

Chief operating officer (30 to 39), financial services company, California

How about getting back to basics—to the "3 R's"? Some of us think this would be a very good idea.

Present teaching methods leave a lot to be desired. We are apparently on a binge to change format from tried and true methods which gave pupils a good foundation on which to build to more sophisticated, "modern" approaches that apparently yield less well-educated individuals. Similarly, the need to question our past practices in the areas of religion, politics, and business has led me to conclude that youth today have no positive direction in which to focus their drives. They seem to be at a loss as to what the future expects of them. They are therefore set adrift with no educational compass and no achievement goals for the most part. This, I believe, is a direct result of the educational morass in which we find ourselves today and from which we must escape. The 3 R's may not have been perfect, but they have stood the test of time as witnessed by the standard of life we know today.

General manager (40 to 49), manufacturing company, Indiana

We need a return to basics. Kids can't do percentages, can't spell, can't write a complete sentence or paragraph. Even graduates of better-known colleges are weak in these areas. People need to know how to read, how to express themselves orally and in writing, and how to perform basic spatial calculations. Specialization is great—a necessity—but on top of fundamentals, not in lieu of them. Forget the preparation for the "human experience" unless you are referring to the real world. There is too much humanizing—too little structure, work, and honest intellectual development.

Executive, personnel and labor relations (40 to 49), food distribution company, New Jersey

Too many high school graduates cannot read, spell, or write legibly. Basic English has been neglected and grammatical errors reflect on the individual's intelligence for life. As service

"Our school system is too oriented toward producing scholars rather than men and women who can be functional citizens."

103

costs continue to mount for household repairs and maintenance, there should be a required course prior to graduation in the simple fundamentals of plumbing, electrical repairs, painting, and gardening. Another required course should cover the American democratic system as compared with other forms of government.

Banker (60 or over), Oregon

A complete overhaul of our educational system is not required. However, I believe that we do need to get back to more emphasis on basic skills (the 3 R's), to find a way to teach individuals interpersonal skills, and how to acquire sound ethical and moral values.

Administrator (40 to 49), educational research laboratory, Pennsylvania

I know that the public schools are teaching English and mathematics. Still, we see many students come to the college level with serious deficiencies in their abilities to read, write, and handle even basic arithmetic. I'm not sure if the cause of these deficiencies lies in what is being taught or how it is being taught. Perhaps a combination of both is involved. But I believe that more emphasis should be placed on the practical use of numbers in teaching mathematics so that students will be able to handle the practical problems they will face as adults. I believe more emphasis should be placed on communications skills in the teaching of English so that students will be able to use the language properly. I believe that much more emphasis needs to be given to teaching students about at least some of the careers open to them, along with a description of the skills they will need to succeed at those careers. We still seem to cling to the idea that education for its own sake is good enough and that it will automatically solve our problems. I guess that I'm saying that much of our educational system needs to return to the basics while still not losing sight of much of the "life-styles" training with which we have become enamored.

Program director and instructor (40 to 49), Texas college

A*re we adequately preparing our young people to live and to earn a living? Some of us can speak from personal experience:*

My experience in educating six children has revealed a very definite decline in the caliber of educators and in the knowledge being imparted to our children. Our children are being taught nothing about the history of our great country. In fact, it is now the "in" thing to ignore the past, to try to forget the present, and to act as if the future will never happen. The new math, for example, has proved a failure. Yet we continue to experiment for the sake of change. Many teachers tell students that they became teachers to avoid going to Vietnam. With these and many other problems, how can we be preparing our youth to effectively deal with reality.

Product marketing manager (40 to 49), pharmaceutical company, Pennsylvania

I definitely do not feel that we are teaching our children to cope and to deal with today's problems and tomorrow's. My own children are going around in circles, being taught to multiply and divide instead of just simply memorizing the multiplication and division tables which they will have to memorize in the end, anyway. It seems that we have to keep a certain number of our educators busy writing new educational programs rather than perfecting the professionalism of our teachers on old programs that have proven reliable. What we have come up with, to date, is a very expensive educational system—which isn't bad, provided we get results. We also get kids who can't read or do simple math or, worse still, who can't make up their own minds.

President (30 to 39), farm
lending cooperative, Illinois

I do not think that our educational system needs a complete overhaul. Much that is taught in schools today does deal with reality, and some courses are very well taught. We do need a system that either strengthens or motivates poor teachers and one that rewards those who really do the job well. A good teacher must not only know and teach her subject well, but she must also be able to convince students that education is worthwhile. My daughter has taught for three years. One course she teaches today is practical math. Students learn how to cope with budgets, bank accounts, the metric system, income taxes, installment buying, and similar practicalities. I get to

correct papers occasionally and am amazed at the depth of thinking developed in some of the students.

Civil engineer (60 or over),
manufacturing plant, Pennsylvania

I am responding to the question on the educational system both as the father of two teen-age boys and as a manager who has been directly and indirectly involved in the hiring of recent high school and college graduates. I do think that we need to do more—starting at the junior high level—to adequately prepare students for the world of work. We also need to better inform students about the various curricula offered in our colleges and the types of jobs they can expect to get based on the curriculum they select. I feel that we need to devote more time to exposing students to the world of work through face-to-face contact with businessmen. Students also need greater exposure to people outside the educational system who are knowledgeable about race relations, government affairs, abortion, and the like. In summary, I'd like to see more emphasis in these areas, but don't feel that we need to throw away our present system.

Manpower planning manager
(40 to 49), natural gas
company, Michigan

"Most vocational guidance counselors are well intentioned but don't know anything to speak of about employment prerequisites, candidate evaluation, and job opportunities."

There is a lot of talk today about the decline of the work ethic. For certain, the world of work is changing in many respects. We want to talk here about some of the ways we believe people's attitudes toward the work they do and how they do it are changing in our country today—for better and for worse.

Productivity is another matter of widespread concern today. Some of us believe it is essential that we increase our national economic output—and soon—if we are to overcome the many challenges—both foreign and domestic—to our economic posture and well-being. Others among us are not so certain that increased productivity alone will be response enough to the serious economic problems we face. Some believe that more fundamental changes in the world of work are called for.

Most of us are in agreement that work-related values and performance in our country are changing. Singled out, however, the contributing factors are many and varied.

THE WORK ETHIC

Once the "work ethic" meant personal and collective striving for betterment. There was pride in accomplishment and a feeling of success and fulfillment as goals were reached. You got what you earned. Now, everything seems to be owed to everyone—people seem to think they are entitled to everything as if by some divine right. There is a built-in satisfaction with mediocrity—a group running away from responsibility—and at the same time a demand to participate and to have authority without accepting responsibility. This is reflected in lower productivity and poorer quality (the Monday and Friday cars from Detroit!).

Increased productivity alone is not the answer to our economic problems. There must be a reeducation in and a reawakening of the principles of "giving" rather than always "taking," of helping others rather than always expecting to be helped (welfare), of individual pride rather than collective guilt. There is nothing inherently evil in participative management and job enrichment, so long as people realize that there is still a boss. We need to reinstill respect for authority in the workplace to achieve order out of chaos.

Corporate officer (40 to 49),
medical services
corporation, Massachusetts

There is something of a disparity between what I grew up to believe was the "work ethic" and the common usage of that term today. The shift from hard work—eight hours of work for eight hours of pay—and the striving to do everything you were told to do to be rewarded has given way to a greater recognition of a person's "self," of his or her innate abilities and the full utilization of them. The other shift we have experienced has grown out of the lack of individual rewards for performance. Equalizing pay on the basis of longevity without regard for performance has led people to ask, "Why work hard? I've got se-

curity and will get the same pay increase as the next guy who goofs off all the time anyway."

Personnel director (30 to 39),
food chain, Alabama

I feel that people today have lost sight of the fact that they can advance themselves socially and economically by taking advantage of educational and training opportunities. It also appears to me that there is a fundamental void in the typical American's understanding of our economic and free enterprise system. There is too much dependence on unions and on governmental agencies. Our modern values are self-defeating in that much of the American work force expects more and more rewards without any noticeable willingness to perform more effectively. In a shrinking world this will limit opportunities for stable employment and consistent prosperity.

Vice president and general
manager (30 to 39),
electrical components
manufacturing company, Ohio

There *is* a decline in the work ethic. Our schools do not adequately prepare young people for meaningful, productive work and neither does our society place enough emphasis on the rewards of hard work. Our "welfare-type" society must be changed if the work ethic is to be improved. Also, unions make unreasonable demands and get what they want because of the power they wield. Legislation must be modified and enforced to restrict unions the way management has been restricted. People must be required to work in order to receive. No one should be guaranteed a standard of living merely by being born.

Treasurer (40 to 49), apparel
manufacturing company, California

There is a definite decline in the work ethic. This is evidenced by the decline in productivity, the increase in absenteeism, higher turnover rates, and poorer quality of work. The situation has been caused by a general lack of interest on the part of individual employees in their jobs and the work they are expected to perform. Job satisfaction is at a very significant low. There is little interest among most workers today in improving performance, because holding a job and being promoted are just not that important. Today, a person can live pretty well and not even work at all. We must change the work environment to make jobs more interesting and find ways to further motivate employees to retain their jobs for economic reasons and as a source of personal satisfaction.

Lawyer (50 to 59), manufacturing company, Minnesota

I believe that our present dedication to computerization ignores the human element in the production of goods and services. The mass of paper, information, and "facts" generated by the computer tends to overwhelm those trying to utilize it and constantly either places people on the defensive or creates personal frustration. Too often the end result is an attitude of "I'll accept anything the computer says." Man, it seems, no longer has anything worth saying. From this, I believe it's obvious that fundamental changes are called for. Perhaps the Volvo and Saab approaches in Sweden can't be universally applied without modification. But at least their findings do indicate that the human element can and must be considered in solving many of our economic problems.

Administrative manager (30 to 39), insurance company, New Jersey

In the past, people worked because there was something in it for them or because they believed in what they were doing. Today, employers can't seem to offer either for most employees. When you take into account food stamps, unemployment insurance, worker's compensation, and other welfare programs and contrast these benefits with high income taxes, inflation, transportation problems, etc., there *isn't* much "in it" any-

more. Also, because we have engineered most of the joy out of most jobs, created a demand for useless products, and established a throwaway economy, the worker has begun to question his own value in industry. Challenging workers to create legitimate and quality goods and services must become industry's first priority.

Personnel director (under 30), general contracting company, Maine

In my opinion the work ethic is not an American ideal per se. The work ethic is merely the expression of a need. In all countries and in all times, people have worked for many different reasons, the most important of which has been the need to obtain the essentials of life—food and shelter. All other needs fade into smoke by comparison. How hard people have been willing to work for these essentials has also varied from time to time and place to place, depending on competition for the available work and the availability of the essentials of life. Thus if food and shelter are inexpensive and easily acquired (and work at comparatively high wages is available), then the need to work will decline and the quality of the work produced will suffer. (This is not to deny that some people for whatever physical or psychological reason will always produce good-quality work at a high volume.)

The one thing that is certain, in my opinion, is that the work ethic has been eroding in the United States for the last 30 years or so at an ever-accelerating pace. I believe that if a scholarly study were made, it would show that the pace of erosion has been directly proportional to the rate of growth of social legislation. The point is, if a person is supplied with basic needs by the government or through union power or other social means, what motivation is left to induce the worker to work? This may seem like a very basic thesis and is certainly contrary to most sociopolitical doctrines in this country today. But if you eliminate all the hoopla and

"Because we have engineered most of the joy out of most jobs, created a demand for useless products, and established a throwaway economy, the worker has begun to question his own value in industry."

bleeding-heart theories, it is the basic reason for the decline in the work ethic.

It has always been my belief that every person should have the opportunity to work as long as he or she exhibits a willingness to work. Certainly those who because of age, illness, or infirmity are unable to work should be supplied with the essentials of life. I believe the work ethic will be restored when the government recognizes that its obligation is not to provide everything for everyone, but only to provide the opportunity to work and to earn those things which people need and desire. All other theories concerning job satisfaction and other reasons for working are nothing more than hogwash.

Businessman (50 to 59), Ohio

I believe that this country is fast approaching a socialistic form of government caused mostly by the make-work nature of most state and federal government jobs. Moreover, the very generous welfare programs created by local, state, and federal governments have had the effect of encouraging job hopping, absenteeism, and other bad attitudes on the part of workers. There is no doubt in my mind that the United States is fast approaching a serious decline in the work ethic, which threatens the free enterprise system that made this country great. I do not believe this trend will reverse itself until the philosophy of government changes and workers are forced to work and to maintain jobs to provide for their own well-being.

Chief executive officer (40 to 49), wood products manufacturing company, North Carolina

The complexity of our society has made it difficult to relate contribution to reward. In previous times, the way we lived was directly related to the effort we put forth. The pioneers knew they had to chop wood to keep warm. They knew that they had to plant and hunt in order to eat. It is very impor-

tant that we devise educational methods that help individuals to better understand their relationship and responsibilities to the society in which they live.

Group vice president (40 to 49), manufacturing company, Illinois

The decline in the work ethic in this country is a problem created by an economy that has been really booming for many years now. The job is a secondary consideration for many Americans. Part of the problem is that many people really do not enjoy the work they do. This is a sad and terrible thing because such a large percentage of people's time is spent on the job. I think that the recession we are experiencing will remind people of the importance of the job and that this attitude will change. The job will be of primary importance, will be more appreciated, and will come to be regarded as more than just a means to an end.

President (60 or over), insurance company, Iowa

I believe the decline of the work ethic is a factor in our adjustment to the machine age. As machines have taken over the bulk of work in industry, man has had to work less to produce more. This is an adaptive process which man has undergone since the beginning of time, and although I think it is an economic shortcoming, it is as natural to man as breathing. In the short run, I believe that increased productivity is the answer to most of our economic problems. By increasing productivity in this country, we can regain jobs lost to foreign nations with cheaper labor, provided the goods produced by our capital-intensive industry can be effectively marketed. In the long run, I believe more fundamental changes are called for. For example, we must begin to examine the social as well as the economic value of the goods and services we produce.

Senior programmer (30 to 39), aerospace company, Pennsylvania

"We must begin to examine the social as well as the economic value of the goods and services we produce."

The work ethic (and rewards) are declining due to assembly-line boredom, no recognition of craftsmanship, and employer "drives" to hire, promote, and overpay lesser qualified minorities. In the absence of labor agreements regarding pay, income rewards fall way below the demands today resulting from increased taxation and inflation—a theft of the individual employee's purchasing power. Other factors affecting a decline in the work ethic include too much government regulation and restriction. Also, there are too many nonproductive elements in the work force, and more and more of these people end up on public payrolls. Welfare costs are out of hand and working people are required to support more and more welfare recipients, who often live better than the workers who take care of them. The public is generally discouraged (low worker morale) due to government waste and political dishonesty. Productivity will not improve until these problems are attacked and overcome.

Health systems specialist
(50 to 59), insurance
company, Massachusetts

"Work ethic" is a term that developed in a period of a strongly accelerating American economy—when it was developing at a rate about equal to the growth of the work force. The work ethic went to hell in the post–World War II era when the economy outstripped the labor supply. During this period management allowed work standards to deteriorate because of the need for "bodies" to keep production up. The reversal of this long-term trend (it's been going on for 30 years now) will be extremely difficult to achieve. A reversal may not even be possible now in view of the prevalent belief in our society that everyone must be taken care of at a level above subsistence.

Assistant division manager
(50 to 59), mining
company, Missouri

Unfortunately, the American people still believe that materialistic growth is the road to success, that the good guy really does come out on top, and that the government serves the will of the people. This, coupled with the thinking that we can get something for nothing—indeed, have the "right" to something for nothing—has led to the corruption of government. The people are deceiving themselves, and those who bolster the deception are able to gain control and authority. People look around and see that others are doing well or at least getting by without being productive, and ask themselves why they should break their backs to provide for themselves and their families and add to the support of the nonproductive. Improving productivity is the answer to the basic problem. It doesn't rest, however, with those who are already productive. The key is to create a society in which all people contribute to the maximum of their productive capacity and continue to be developed in ways that will assure the maximization of their capabilities and productivity.

Plant manager (40 to 49),
industrial products
company, Mississippi

I have observed a polarization of "doers" and "nondoers." "Doers" work hard and expect rewards. "Nondoers" don't work hard and still expect rewards. Our system does not seem to penalize "nondoers," and the trend toward socialization in America encourages them.

Controller (30 to 39),
manufacturing and distribution
company, New Jersey

If our prices are too high to be acceptable to ourselves and our foreign customers, it is perhaps much less a consequence of a "decline in the work ethic" than the predictable result of 40 years of governmental actions that have directly or indirectly forced selling prices upward. I would enjoy entering any marketplace with any American product that did not have to contain in its selling price the markups needed to cover the nonproductive activities ordered, sponsored, or encouraged by our government. When will we realize that legislative requirements are the single greatest factor affecting our place in the world economy today? When will we accept the fact that industrial prosperity is both a function of national thrift and the basic requirement for national security and an improvement in the quality of life?

Vice president, engineering (50 to 59), agri-business company, Minnesota

Youth is disillusioned with the world today. Youth takes no pride in doing a job well. This is perhaps due to too much mechanization in work methods. Maybe we should revert to the craftsman system that allowed people to be more creative and imaginative.

Personnel manager (40 to 49), publishing company, Pennsylvania

The younger generation today seems to have less dedication to the job than was the case in the past. I don't know whether this is an expression of more self-interest or whether it is the result of more employment opportunities which, of course, provide greater economic security. What I do know is that there is almost a feverish desire among the young today for quick promotion and increased compensation. This compares with the old ethic of feeling that a job well done over a period of time would eventually result in career success.

Attorney and retired bank vice president and trust officer (60 or over), Ohio

A very great problem in the world of work today is the increasingly adversary relationship between the leaders of labor and management. We have constructed a highly complex economic system in which the management of labor and the welfare of labor are separately institutionalized concerns. We need a new school of thought—a new professional discipline—that embraces simultaneously the interests and functions of management *and* labor. We need to bring all these separate interests together under one roof if we are to be economically successful in the new world economic order that is taking shape. It's true that a house divided cannot stand—not anymore.

President (40 to 49), New York university

Workers today—because of union influence—do not consider themselves a part of the company they work for. Workers try to find ways not to work or to get paid for time not worked. This reduces productivity. Workers today do not take pride in their work, and product quality has declined as a result. Government has added to the dilemma by enacting EEO laws and attendant regulations. Companies cannot discriminate on the basis of sex, age, creed, national origin, and the like. Employers must hire the handicapped, females, and minorities—regardless of ability. It seems it's becoming more and more important to establish a good EEO record. Matters of ability and hard work have become secondary.

Secretary and treasurer (50 to 59), sales and engineering company, Ohio

I'm convinced that most people generally have a positive attitude toward their work. If they are given the opportunity to learn a job and are acquainted with the acceptable standards of performance, they will usually measure up. Our biggest shortcoming in indus-

"We have constructed a highly complex economic system in which the management of labor and the welfare of labor are separately institutionalized concerns. . . . It's true that a house divided cannot stand —not anymore."

trial mass production jobs (the assembly line) today is the lack of clearly defined and attainable job standards. Pressure to meet production schedules—many times at the expense of quality—has a negative impact, in the long run, on employee attitudes toward the job, the supervisor, and the company. We must reexamine the prime motivating factor in private enterprise—the "maximization of profits"—especially in view of changing attitudes generally. Sacrificing workers to welfare rolls so as to maintain or achieve immorally high profits has a debilitating impact on our entire society.

Director of employee relations (40 to 49), multinational corporation, New York

Some of us believe that the work ethos fostered by organized labor has contributed significantly to current woes in the workplace.

I believe that the biggest single reason for the decline of the work ethic is the "Big Brother" approach used by unions. Collective bargaining units are now commonplace among such "ex-professionals" as teachers, policemen, and many middle management groups. In particular, younger workers seem to have been raised with a philosophy that if something is too difficult, their parents will take care of it. In the business world, parents have been replaced by the union. If tomorrow's leaders are to lead, they must act responsibly, reliably, independently, and with good old-fashioned initiative and self-pride. Otherwise, it will be just a matter of "attrition" before today's economic system in America disappears.

Vice president (30 to 39),
clothing manufacturing
company, Pennsylvania

The concept of what constitutes a day's work has declined among all too many employees today. More pay for less work has become the norm, especially among unionized employees who are protected from discharge even when they produce poorly. Collective bargaining for wages and salaries and benefits far beyond those justified by productivity increases per employee has helped to create an adversary environment. Selfishness rules the day. To get everything possible for the union employee—regardless of the effect on the organization, its customers, and the general public—seems to be the goal of unions today. In a recent strike in our company, our union workers took a completely callous attitude toward the hardships being suffered by those members of our community who were without electric service as a result of their job action.

Operating manager (60 or over),
electric utility, California

I feel that people's attitude toward work has undergone a significant change since World War II. Some of this change has been positive as workers seem to be more independent and generally more aware of their roles in the work force and in society. I do feel, however, that with this increased awareness has come a great misunderstanding of one aspect of the work ethic: the degree to which a worker should share in the profits. It seems that virtually all organized labor groups (including teachers, policemen, sanitation workers, athletes, etc.) want to extract as much as possible from their respective organizations without regard for any objective job criteria such as education, training, responsibility, job skills, and the like. I feel that this pronounced tendency toward gouging has created a marked imbalance in our whole economic system. Labor groups are no longer paid on the basis of job skills or requirements, but on the basis of how much clout they can muster against their employers. Productivity improvements can certainly help the situation, but the only effective solution is a fundamental change in the work environment that fosters fair and equitable wages based on objective economic criteria—not "political" pressure.

Manager of industrial engineering
(40 to 49), manufacturing
company, Pennsylvania

While many of us believe that employee attitudes are at fault, a Kansas executive thinks dull jobs are the culprit—that the decline of the "work ethic" is a myth.

I think that the decline of the work ethic is a myth. People have always disliked hard, boring jobs, but few people have had a choice until recent decades. I believe that the question of work ethics only arises in a situation where people have the choice to work or not to work. If people can get enough money to survive without working, it's not surprising that many choose not to work if available jobs are dull, tedious, or physically exhausting. If the work ethic is important (and I'm not sure it is), we must create jobs that are more fulfilling for the people who have to do them. If we don't mechanize dull jobs or redesign them to be more challenging, there is little hope, in my opinion, that the American work ethic will improve.

> *Executive (30 to 39), life insurance company, Kansas*

People's attitude toward work has changed for the worse. There is a lack of commitment and a lack of any feeling of responsibility among workers today. Very few workers have a sense of pride in their work. This is the result of a total lack of discipline in the home, in our schools, in the courts and in the national government. Until we get back to the basics of training our young people in the right manner and with the right discipline instead of letting them do "their own thing," the situation will not improve.

> *President (30 to 39), aerial mapping company, Illinois*

I am convinced that a majority of people today do not particularly like the work they do, don't do it particularly well, and aren't overly concerned about improving the situation. Moreover, I think we are getting used to this sorry state of affairs which sub-

stitutes unreasoning demands for individual initiative. Productivity based on the work ethic never was a final solution to economic problems, but the forthrightness, honesty, loyalty, and thrift fostered by it were critical to our sense of social responsibility. Somehow, within the pattern of change—possibly by providing for greater worker participation in decision making and by increasing responsibility—we must again instill in people the pride and sense of achievement lacking in the world of work today.

> *Architect (50 to 59), multidiscipline planning company, Iowa*

What better proof is there of a decline in the work ethic than the performance level of most workers and the results of their labor? Both are shoddy today and indicate an indifference to the job. This is a direct result of no appreciation for excellence on the part of so many people—both adolescents and adults. Just about everyone today seems to be satisfied with mediocrity. Merely improving productivity is not the solution to this problem. Something within the work environment must change if worker attitudes are to improve. A sense of accomplishment and pride must once again become a part of the work situation. Failing this, the work ethic will continue to deteriorate.

> *Director of labor relations (50 to 59), manufacturing company, Illinois*

Young people (in the 10 to 17 age group) are not taught how to derive real satisfaction out of doing a job well. Such satisfaction can be a real pleasure and can make an otherwise tedious (or intolerable) job actually

fun. This satisfaction works better than raw willpower in helping a person work a hard job through to completion and still do a good job.

> *President (50 to 59), consulting company, Maryland*

I certainly feel that people are not as productive today as yesterday and that there is not nearly as much pride in accomplishment. I have noticed the difference after coming out of almost 15 years of retirement to return to federal service. Productivity improvement without a corresponding grass roots realization of fundamental work values (the work ethic) is not the answer. I believe that we must make an effort to revitalize our moral and social structures as we try to find ways to increase productivity.

> *Logistical manager (50 to 59), U.S. Army, Puerto Rico*

I don't believe there's any question that there has been a decline in the work ethic. In my opinion, the contributing factors—not necessarily in order of significance—are (1) the strength and power of unions, (2) Watergate and other scandals both in business and in the public sector, (3) the politics of "Big Business," and (4) the selfish interests of many, if not most, people today ("I come first! The company and my associates are not very important!"). Combined with these is the strong desire to make as much money in as short a time as possible—no matter what it takes to do so. Merely improving productivity is not the answer to our economic woes. We must reinstill a sense of pride in people.

> *Area financial director (30 to 39), sales company, New York*

People living in today's society no longer, for the most part, take pride in their work. Years ago, a person was given a raise because he deserved it. He did the job he was assigned to do to the best of his ability, continuously trying to improve on ways to be more efficient and more effective. Management rewarded this behavior by increasing the worker's salary on the basis of individual contribution. Today, 2,000 workers receive an increase in salary because they belong to a labor union. Most workers no longer take pride in their work and, in my opinion, have lost sight of whom they work for and why they are working.

*Vice president and treasurer
(40 to 49), public warehousing
company, Ohio*

The work ethic has gradually changed. Over a period of years the Christian ethic of "work hard and you will be rewarded" has, for the most part, diminished in influence. Ever-increasing welfare rolls, unemployment benefits, unionism, etc., have reduced individual incentive. Work for self-satisfaction, pride in accomplishment, and doing or making something better for its own sake have become rarities. Too often money alone is the prime motivation for working. As a result, pride in oneself is something that many and probably most people do not even understand. If, somehow, more people could understand the true meaning of the word "contribution," they would have a fuller and happier time and others would benefit and also learn, hopefully, to give of themselves to the job. Then productivity would take care of itself.

*President (40 to 49),
office products
distribution company, Ohio*

M*anagement policies and practices are also in part responsible for many of the current problems of the workplace—and management has its work cut out for it if conditions are to improve.*

One of the major reasons for a decline in the work ethic is that we as managers have failed to make certain that every employee understands what is expected of him. Managers have a responsibility to make sure that every employee understands how good work performance will allow the individual worker to attain some of his or her personal goals in the long run.

*Assistant personnel manager
(50 to 59), electric
utility, New York*

The work environment is constantly changing due to increased technology, service, and competition. In addition, workers are also changing. But the work ethic remains a driving force and a need within individuals, and the environment must provide a proper climate to stimulate, motivate, and utilize the capabilities that individual workers bring to business. Most workers do have a desire to learn, and management must respond to that desire rather than trying to depress it through a work climate and management styles more appropriate to the 1930s and 1940s. I believe that management must also be more aware of the fact that due to the affluence most people enjoy, there are many other areas of life into which workers can direct their energies. This—coupled with the fact that most people spend the major portion of their day at the plant or office—should reinforce the idea that management must provide a proper climate to stimulate and motivate productivity.

*Vice president, personnel
and management development
(30 to 39), bank holding
company, Massachusetts*

The decline of the work ethic is the result of the labor force maturing faster than the organizations that employ people. People's attitudes toward work have not changed—work is still work! What has changed is the blind willingness among people to enthusiastically perform a job that is viewed as "work." Unfortunately, improving productivity is a very short-run solution to our economic problems. Until we see a growth in the "people ethic" by organizations, productivity increases will be limited to those made possible by mechanical technology.

Management development consultant
(30 to 39), petrochemical
company, Oklahoma

Because people no longer work solely to keep body and soul together, they seek greater personal fulfillment in their vocation. This demands more of the organization in terms of developing individual creativity. While accomplishment can and must be measured in terms of productivity, the worth of a job is more and more important to people today. A feeling of personal worth and the contribution their efforts make to society are the things people now respond to. The organization that can harness these feelings has nothing to fear.

Internal auditor (50 to 59),
communications company, Alabama

The worker's attitude is changing for the worse. Productivity is down per man-hour. Lack of interest in satisfying quality standards is appalling—not only on the part of the worker, but more so among manufacturers. The attitude that "this is as good as we can do with the available work force" is rampant among most manufacturers. Go into the marketplace and purchase almost any product. How trouble-free is it today? In short, what can we expect from workers when we in management have such a complacent attitude?

Marketing director (50 to 59),
furniture manufacturing
company, Tennessee

The work ethic may not be declining, but radical changes have taken place. These changes have been influenced by increased educational levels, the changing composition of the labor force, affluence, the psychology of entitlement, and a much younger, better-informed employee population —in short, younger, smarter, more vocal individuals protected by endless legal provisions and the media. Workers are concerned with their "rights" today, and their attitudes differ from those of people who were "lucky to have a job" during the 1930s. Leadership responsibilities in business today include making jobs more meaningful—thus making full use of the talents, abilities, interests, and time of all employees. Companies are concerned with the return on investment in human time, and the changing work ethic is now demanding a return on investment for the time invested by the individual in the company. It is perhaps in the area of individual expectations that the greatest change in employee/employer relationships will occur during the remainder of the twentieth century.

Vice president, personnel
(50 to 59), department
store chain, North Carolina

A sense of involvement is essential to employee satisfaction and improved productivity, in our estimation.

In the past, people were motivated by the threat of hunger and asked few questions. Today, the fear of hunger doesn't motivate Americans. Yet American business still largely attempts to "buy" workers. Worker commitment must be earned by sharing management and by involving people in decision making. Also, management must start to reward workers in a personal way and on a daily basis. This will require a higher integrity than most managers possess. Managers must commit themselves to the welfare of their employees as well as to the welfare of the company and learn to love and respect employees as equals. Only a joint commitment by workers and management will help to improve American productivity.

Management consultant
(40 to 49), Georgia

With the growth of organizations, sociologists have developed techniques to motivate workers without really getting them involved in meaningful ways. In fact, involvement and responsibility have become dirty words in life today—and particularly in business. Instead of continuing to develop sophisticated "noninvolvement" motivational techniques, managers today need to practice "cornfield politics." Get out among the workers, get to know them, drink with them, break bread with them, get to know their hopes and fears. This kind of intimate, direct contact is beneficial. Without it, we will continue to build a structured hierarchy of classes in the work force (and in society) that will one day destroy all that so many have given so much to achieve.

Developer (30 to 39),
hospital management
corporation, Maryland

People's attitude toward work is changing for the worse. It's difficult today to find an employee who feels that the work he or she is doing is important or that he or she personally is important to the overall work and success of the company. A big part of the problem is that we have spent the past 25 years creating conflict groups both in society at large and in the work environment. Unless this condition is reversed and employees are once again made to feel that they are important and share responsibility for organizational success, our entire democratic system is threatened. My main concern is that future increases in productivity will create additional conflict between management and labor. Today, conflict exists not only between management and organized labor, but in all areas of the labor force.

Senior partner (50 to 59),
accounting firm, New Jersey

I believe that fundamental changes in the work environment are necessary. Work is important and natural to man—yet it must be meaningful work that one can get involved in. I believe that much needs to be done to better match people to the kinds of jobs they can get "turned on" to.

Associate professor of business
(30 to 39), Oklahoma university

One of us believes that the decline of the work ethic may spell the destruction of our civilization, while others see positive effects as well.

The decline in the work ethic is real and apparent. Whether that is good or bad depends on one's point of view. Personally I find it refreshing. For the first time people are realizing that work is not an end in itself and that there are other, more important things in life such as self-fulfillment, family, friends, etc. This realization is being forced upon people because of the stratification of responsibilities. No longer do we have craftsmen who shepherd products from inception to their final disposition. Unfortunately, the majority of workers today are subjected to assembly-line conditions in one form or another.

Product manager (30 to 39),
chemical manufacturing
company, Illinois

117

The decline of the work ethic has become very real in recent years. This is evidenced not only by decreased productivity but also by shoddy workmanship in the construction field and in most of the products we manufacture. While there are a few exceptions, most people no longer take pride in the work they do and in doing their work well. Most people are only interested in more pay for less work so that they can spend more time in leisure activities. The attitude of "what's in it for me?" will eventually destroy our civilization if it continues.

Marketing analyst (40 to 49),
railroad, Minnesota

I believe the big change in employee attitudes toward work is that more people want to be working at what they enjoy. They want to receive personal satisfaction from the work they do rather than just doing what their employer thinks is best. This change is the result of better educational opportunities, greater job opportunities, and more enlightened management. Employees produce much more in a job situation they like and find the work more challenging and personally rewarding.

Vice president, employee and
community relations (50 to 59),
credit corporation, Connecticut

Many people today believe that life has no meaning and purpose save those which we lend to it—that life is nothing more than what *we* make of it, that the best and noblest of our earthly works serve no purpose higher than our own.

But most of us clearly disagree with this notion. Some suggest that life's meaning and purpose are for Divine Providence alone to know and understand, while others feel certain that the meaning and purpose of our individual lives will be revealed to us if we will but set aside our own small ideas and ambitions and seek God's guidance and instruction in all that we think about and do. God, many believe, has plans and purposes for all of His creations, and all His plans are good and perfect. The trouble with the world may be that too many of us have too many plans of our own.

THE MEANING, PURPOSE, AND AIM OF LIFE

"I believe that many people are finding that personal and family development are much more satisfying and productive than competition for social or job success."

I do not agree that life has no meaning and purpose save those which we lend to it. I believe in God and my existence is to give greater honor and glory to Him. As I do this, so I will receive eternal reward. My life does add to the definition or level of accomplishment of the purpose, however.

Business manager (40 to 49), public school district, New York

My life has meaning because of my personal faith in the Lord Jesus Christ who is "the power of God unto salvation to every one that believeth; to the Jew first, and also to the Greek" (Romans 1:16). My life has purpose because I have a share in proclaiming the gospel of Christ to many people in order that they, too, may share in the abundant life which the Lord Jesus will give to any who receive Him as Lord and Savior. I have an inner peace that cannot be taken from me. Though all else may fail, He never fails. I have proven this through times of adversity as well as in times of prosperity. May God bless you.

Cemetery manager (60 or over), Illinois

Jesus Christ gives all meaning and purpose to life no matter what you lend to it.

Personnel manager (under 30), Pennsylvania bank

Life has a meaning beyond what I "lend" to it. I was created by God and He through His Holy Spirit controls my life. Through His life and resurrection I am assured of eternal life now and after death. Through His guidance my life has purpose and what I do each day is a reflection of His purpose for me. Certainly this has put a meaning in my life and I try to control my activities with His guidance.

Vice president, administration (50 to 59), public utility, Texas

I disagree with this idea completely. I realize that what I am about to say may sound religious, but it has brought meaning and purpose into my life. I do believe that truth has to come from a positive outside source. I believe that that positive outside source is God. I believe God created human beings for the purpose of having companionship with them. The Bible says in John 3:16, "For God so loved the world that He gave His only Son so that anyone who believes in Him shall not perish but have eternal life." The purpose of my life is to get other people to realize that there is more to life than existing 60, 70, or 80 years and then it's all over. Rather, death is just the beginning to an eternity with God and His Son Jesus Christ. Having a goal which is higher than one's own personal ambition brings meaning to my life.

Manager (40 to 49), bakery supply company, California

I disagree with the idea that life has no meaning and purpose save those which people lend to it. I firmly believe that the meaning and purpose of life are something greater than we, as individuals, can measure. True, each one of us was placed on this earth to make certain contributions. However, individual contributions would not be meaningful unless they became a part of the total contribution made by others. Life is short and what sometimes appears to be no contribution may end up becoming the most important contribution—either by raising children or participating in the educational, cultural, civic, or business life of our communities and our country. Each day offers a challenge, and we should meet these challenges to the best of our ability. If we do, life has a "meaning" and a "purpose."

Vice president, administration (60 or over), public utility, Washington

I disagree. Life has meaning and purpose whether we lend them to it or not. That is, we may be accomplishing a purpose even when we think we are not. Many of the purposes our lives serve, I feel, are in this category.

Systems analyst (30 to 39), aerospace components company, Arizona

I disagree. I think that life does have meaning and purpose and does not depend on what any particular group of individuals lends to it. If one considers that the main purpose of life is to glorify God and to honor Him and that He is all-powerful, then there is much meaning to life. The history of this country and the world is filled with the ups and downs of civilization and with periods of recession and depression and good times. This country is a great country because of the free enterprise system and because of the natural resources and the type of government that makes free enterprise operate. I believe the economic and political downturn we are now in will be beneficial in the long run, even though people's misunderstanding of economic facts will demand an extravagant government. But the efforts of the people will be powerful enough to correct our economic and political system. This country, while changing, will move forward. Our belief in God as a people and our acknowledgment of Him are the important factors that will make this nation the great land that it is.

President (60 or over), life insurance company, Tennessee

I disagree with the concept that life has no meaning. We were placed on the earth for some purpose. Each individual must set his or her own objectives and goals and work toward an end. Each individual decides his or her own future, meanings, and concepts for thinking. We must think positively in all our undertakings. The best advice is that if you don't succeed the first time, try, try again until success is your reward.

Technical information retriever (30 to 39), Indiana

People who do believe that life has no purpose are purely ignorant of why we exist. All answers to living are given to us in the Bible, which is our guide to the very brief period of time on this great earth. People tend to forget the fortunes (spiritual and material) that can be obtained by giving and not always expecting something in return. A bad past experience is a challenge. If only we can all be good forgetters, we would vividly discover that the successful person forgets past experiences, cannot afford to look behind, and the magnanimous man forgets because he is too big to let little things disturb him. I live on the basis of being a good forgetter because business dictates it and success demands it. It is still a beautiful world.

Vice president and general manager (30 to 39), data processing company, Pennsylvania

I agree that life has no meaning and purpose save those which I lend to it. The most meaningful and satisfying rewards one can experience are from giving or lending to others. Giving or lending may be in many forms—creating a new machine needed by industry or society, painting, music, writing. Also through philanthropic giving, one is satisfied and one's life purpose is rewarded. Giving and lending also give purpose to life.

President (60 or over), farm equipment manufacturing company, Kansas

I do not agree that life has no meaning and purpose except what I lend to it. A brief look at any aspect of life around us—whether it be in the world of the smallest creature to the stars in the sky—can lead to but one conclusion: that we are all part of a huge master plan as established by God. Accordingly, while we all may contribute in our everyday lives to our own present-day happiness and the happiness of others, there is a meaning and purpose which have been basically structured as a part of the master plan, within which we are all contained.

Vice president (50 to 59), engineering and construction company, Massachusetts

I strongly disagree that life has no purpose except what we lend to it. I believe in God, and I believe He gives purpose to life beyond us. I derive my personal goals in life from what I believe He wants me to do and find a great deal of personal pleasure in the work I do.

Physician (30 to 39), private practice, Georgia

I agree with this idea. There is great emphasis on the pursuit of material things and comforts. Yet the only satisfaction in life can be derived from the interpersonal relationships we develop—be they with family or others. Our culture does not seem to encourage or nurture this as is done, I believe, in the Italian and Chinese family, for example.

Corporate planner (50 to 59), food processing company, Pennsylvania

I agree with the belief that life has no meaning and purpose save those which people lend to it. Meaning and purpose cannot be some esoteric goal or hope expected at some future instant in time. It cannot be given by another person or organization. Our social, economic, political, and religious institutions and their members can only provide opportunities for individuals

to lead meaningful and purposeful lives. But each person must participate in the area most suitable for him or her, and the rewards will be in direct proportion to the effort put forth.

Manager (40 to 49), California company

Our observed purpose in life would have to relate to what we "lend" or put into it. It could not be otherwise, even if one's viewpoint were so limited that one found nothing identifiable through which to contribute.

Senior vice president, operations (40 to 49), savings and loan association, Colorado

If I understand this idea correctly, then I agree. The meaning and purpose of life must be within each individual and may be substantially different from person to person. In my experience, one had better not look for life's meaning through the eyes of another human, else he may be terribly disillusioned and unfulfilled. Religion, for some, may offer some guidance with respect to meaning and purpose, but ultimately all must find meaning and purpose within. This seems to me the only rational answer.

Division manager (40 to 49), construction company, Nevada

Life is what an individual makes of it. If one puts little into improving the conditions around him and does not show love and concern for others, he will get little out of life. Life can be full and happy if man will love man instead of the conveniences of our way of life. Christ came to serve man, so must man serve his fellow man if he is to be complete and happy. You will get out of life what you put into it.

Chief financial officer
(40 to 49), bank holding
company, Texas

Life has no meaning since our values are different from country to country—or even within a given country. Psychic needs are not satisfied for most people in materially satisfied societies.

Manufacturing manager
(30 to 39), Illinois company

I agree. Life is just whatever the individual chooses it to be, but always a dynamic experience and extremely personal. Life is, for me, my stream of conscious awareness, my perceptual, emotional, intellectual, and striving processes. I recognize that some people have highly conditioned defensive processes which involve beliefs, attitude sets, biases, prejudices, inhibitions, and so forth. I guess that people make of life what they feel to be necessary for their own emotional/physical security. Life essentially is ludicrous, meaningless, and becomes whatever the individual is fortunate enough to make of it for himself. Some people find it necessary or desirable to interpret life as some magical, mystical "thing" that transcends them and is directed by some power beyond their ken or control. Such a view removes people from being in responsible control of their experience, and substitutes guilt, fear, and anxiety for joy and self-actualization.

University professor and
consulting psychologist
(30 to 39), California

I agree with this belief because I believe we all define the meaning of life in terms of our own experience and needs.

Training specialist (30 to 39),
state agency, New York

I agree. This allows one to take an independent and individualistic approach to life. If there were any meaning or purpose to life defined by any real or superficial entity other than oneself, then life would be a form of slavery. Besides, in my own life so far, I haven't seen any convincing evidence to lead me to believe otherwise.

Consultant, financial planning
and control (under 30), New York

I don't believe that very many people today literally believe that life has no meaning and purpose save those which they lend to it—though many people may feel so. To say that life has no meaning or purpose is an emotional expression of despair or frustration, rather than a statement of rational thought. It seems to me that if an individual says that he or she "lends meaning and purpose to life," there has to first be an admission that there are such qualities. If there aren't, then no one can "lend" them. I do believe that many people are (1) unwilling to invest of themselves to find meaning and purpose, or, most likely (2) already have some inkling of it and are afraid to learn more because of the demands and responsibilities they have to place on themselves as a result.

Manager, data processing division
(40 to 49), agricultural
supply cooperative, Kansas

I think purpose is "lent" by attempting to develop in oneself (and by working to enable others to develop in themselves) full potential for self-expression and fulfillment. It becomes difficult as values change and doubly important to avoid the laying of values on people in this development process. I've certainly had to reevaluate my own values to enable the developmen-

tal process to work in both my own staff (at work) and my teen-age children. Seeing the growth which occurs verifies my commitment, and from this I gain a sense of purpose in my life.

Staff development director
(40 to 49), county social
service department, California

The absence today of strong prevailing political, moral, or spiritual values and leadership for those values—added to a predominantly materialistic philosophy in our society—leaves no other alternative but to identify with the nuclear or immediate family as the anchor for meaning and purpose in life.

Hospital administrator
(40 to 49), Minnesota

Like anything else, life depends on the individual. You get out of life what you put into it. If you are positive and realistic, you reap positive and realistic rewards. If you are negative and unrealistic, then you are disappointed by the results. You live best when you can live with yourself. Too many people live in the future or in the past, rather than living one day at a time to the best of their ability.

Vice president, industrial
relations (40 to 49),
New Jersey company

I believe life does have a significant meaning. I think it depends to a large extent on our objectives and our goals as individuals. I think that people who are self-oriented and look strictly for personal gratification are sometimes disillusioned if their energies are not channeled into activities that they feel are contributing to the well-being of others. I believe this is particularly true in my occupational field, in that banking does provide a very creative opportunity in the promotion of the well-being of the community and its people. The significance of contributions may not always be as evident as we would like, but should certainly be enough to believe privately that one's life has meaning and that when you are no longer alive, the country, community, and the institution you worked for are better off for your having been here than had you never been here at all.

President (30 to 39),
Arkansas bank

We are all born with a physiological module. This module allows us to operate with a given range of awareness, capability, and productivity. It should be our purpose—and is my purpose—to maximize my performance within the physiological range that I inherited. The payoff is in the knowledge of having done one's best and in the luxury of occasionally seeing the benefits of one's efforts.

Vice president, marketing
(50 to 59), machinery
manufacturing company, California

"The Great Authority" says, "You shall have no other Gods before Me," and "You shall love your neighbor as yourself." On those two commandments hangs man's destiny. Measure yourself by them honestly. Measure anyone or any action by them to determine the meaning and purpose of life. Our concern with "self" and our "selfishness" is probably our greatest weakness today. Some will say this is an oversimplification, but I say not. Can anyone suggest anything better?

Purchasing manager (50 to 59),
food processing company,
state not indicated

The lack of a real purpose in life is especially evident in young people today in the 18 to 24 age group. The cause is probably multifaceted, but it seems to me that high on the list is the pace of change we are witnessing today and the general lack of self-reliance. There is a strong feeling that if one belongs to enough groups, someone in some of them will take care of one's problems and one will not have to face the issues oneself. Perhaps young people—or some of

them—have had things too easy and need to stretch more and rely on themselves for more. Young people lack an adequate set of values; they lack a true perspective for living, and do not know the joy in accomplishment, in creating, and in demonstrating to others what they can do.

Professor (60 or over),
Indiana university

The quality of life has become increasingly important to my family and me, and material and job success have become much less important in recent years. Our spiritual growth, emotional health, and family social activities are areas of development which we are especially enjoying. I believe that many people are finding that personal and family development are much more satisfying and productive than competition for social or job success.

Director of research and
development (40 to 49),
hospital association, Minnesota

Life has a meaning. I have been placed here by the Lord to serve and glorify Him.

Engineer (40 to 49), electric
power supply company, Colorado

T*o talk about the aim of life is to talk about what we are living for—to what ends we are directing our energies, to what ends we are devoting our time.*

We are placed on earth to undergo a series of experiences in order to learn certain lessons. The harder and more bitter the lesson, the quicker we learn. The sooner we learn to face each new experience with the questioning attitude of, "Where is the lesson to be learned?" rather than "Why me?" the quicker we gain relief from the misery of these experiences. Over a period of time our philosophy of life begins to evolve and we appreciate those truly nice things that happen to us, and our positive attitude toward lessons and experiences begins to pay dividends in terms of better-quality service and better mental and physical health. Over a period of time, our reaction to life's problems becomes much more logical and sensible, and we begin to respond in a more intelligent manner. Consequently, once we discover the "aim of life"—which is service—then the meaning and purpose become evident.

Director of personnel
(30 to 39), Oklahoma hospital

In my view, the aim of life is to leave the world (particularly the human condition) in better shape than I found it.

Manager (40 to 49), research
and development organization,
New Hampshire

I can only speak for my personal aim which, incidentally, I hope is not too much different from that of most Americans: (1) to get an education to prepare myself for a productive, meaningful life; (2) to support my family comfortably and to give my children the opportunity to get an education so that they might be useful to someone else besides themselves; (3) to serve God and my community; (4) to find pride and contentment in doing my job efficiently but not without feeling; (5) to save enough money for my wife and me to live comfortably without being a burden on the children after they have established their families and after we have retired; and (6) to contribute

"The sooner we learn to face each new experience with the questioning attitude of, 'Where is the lesson to be learned?' rather than 'Why me?' the quicker we gain relief from the misery of these experiences."

significantly toward making the world a better place to live in than it would have been had I not lived.

Executive director (50 to 59), hospital, Illinois

The aim of life is to live in accordance with the laws or principles which govern human existence and which move human life along toward its natural outcome or transformation. In a real sense the process is the end and the end is the process, for the process is infinite and without end. The prime principle which governs human existence and which fuels the life process for human beings is the force called "love." Scientists have other words for this force or principle. For the most part we have not discovered the other laws and follow the love principle only halfheartedly, at best.

Personnel consultant (30 to 39), charitable organization, New York

In secular language, the aim of life is to live out one's inner creativity in behalf of values that enhance human worth and community and to participate in changing the institutions that bear, affect, and enhance these values in, through, and beyond all the stresses involved in doing so. In terms of faith, the aim of life is to be a person of hope who gives hope to others in and through a ministry of love.

Pastor of Presbyterian congregation (50 to 59), Indiana

The aim of life is to enjoy the experience of living, to survive the perils of living, and to ensure the continuation of the human species.

Management engineer (50 to 59), hospital, Virginia

The aim of life is to prepare for afterlife, the hereafter. Then and there—wherever—will come the ultimate reckoning. Then we will be held accountable for that which during life we have been responsible—ourselves, our earthly associates, our family, friends, co-workers, and others, our share of our society and its institutions. If we

believe this and try to live this, we will attain self-realization and the warmth of satisfaction in constructive accomplishment will be felt. We will sense the rewards—temporal and infinite—of service to others. We are all imperfect teachers, but we may be forgiven if we have advanced the matter a little and have done our best.

Assistant medical director (50 to 59), steel producing company, Pennsylvania

I have learned that God loves us, has a plan for our lives, and can guarantee our salvation after death. The acceptance of Christ into my life by faith has caused me to turn from my old ways of doing things and to commit my life to living for Christ. Living for the Lord is my purpose and the Bible is my life's guideline. This is "heart" knowledge of God. A commitment to Christ by faith alone is the only way we can have "the abundant life."

Administrative assistant (under 30), oil field construction company, Montana

To know one's self.

Budget analyst (under 30), city budget division, Illinois

The aim of life is to plan and work toward a life that is filled with contentment, happiness, and fullness in work and play. If this is not now the case—change it.

Administrator (under 30), medical university, South Carolina

The aim of life is various things to various people. I would define it in my life as my view on who I am, where I fit into society and where I want to fit in, and the mode through which I plan to reach that station. Basically, I would correlate it with being at Point X and "aiming" for Point Y. The interesting part is how fast I want to get there, and do I walk, crawl, drive, travel first-class or economy?

Accounting department manager (under 30), insurance company, Massachusetts

If one were to attempt to define the aim of life, he would have to expound on all that he would expect to put into his own life for the attainment of his own personal goals. He would also have to expound on the means he would hope and try to use in reaching these ends.

Senior administrative assistant (under 30), retail merchandising company, Illinois

Like a meandering river, the course of our lives, from the cradle to the grave, is often blocked by different barriers. Too often, we choose to go around them rather than face up to the challenges with which life confronts us. This tendency to avoid the reality of our situation has become almost habitual as, more and more, the need for material growth has taken precedence over our commitment to self-development and spiritual growth. We have been taught to believe that the aim of life lies somewhere at the end of the long road to material success. Barriers are often pockets of truth—something we cannot easily understand—and if we stop to take the time to overcome them, the fear of others passing us by becomes so great that we usually opt to sidestep them and learn little or nothing about our lives. This I know: two people are born and die at precisely the same moment; both have traveled the same distance; one added ''quantity'' to life by constantly sidestepping; the other added ''quality'' by maintaining a direct path and doing what had to be done.

Placement counselor (under 30), personnel agency, New York

The aim of life is to be happy doing whatever it is that you want to do while contributing to the benefit of others or at least not injuring them. Life to me simply means existence, and people must individually find what is meaningful to them. For me, my religion gives my life a lot of its meaning—a belief in a life after death, the level of which is based on the good deeds I do while on earth. No man is an island. Love is nothing unless sacred. People need other people and we should each take it upon ourselves to improve the lives of the people with whom we come in contact.

Senior manager (30 to 39), computer processing services company, New York

The ''aim of life'' is that which an individual places above all others in terms of priorities through his actions rather than his words. The most worthy aim for all is to achieve that which his Maker intended for him when He created him. That aim, I believe, can only be achieved through a personal relationship with Jesus Christ, our Maker's Son, and only by living as directed by the Holy Spirit. God's will for a man's life is developed and revealed to him step by step.

Vice president (30 to 39), oil and gas servicing company, Oklahoma

The aim of life is (1) to survive, (2) to maintain a rational balance, (3) to accept change, (4) to retain enthusiasm for whatever one does in business or outside of business, and (5) to enjoy the world.

Partner (30 to 39), accounting firm, New York

The aim of life is to make a sincere and significant contribution to your particular field of endeavor. By ''sincere,'' I mean total contribution of talent and energy dedicated to achieving success. By ''significant,'' I mean a real, creative achievement in the field that took individual courage to pursue and make work. If a person's aim in life is just to survive, then he or she will attain nothing more than mediocrity. If a person's aim in life is to meet any and all challenges, then it will take the above definition and a real ''leader'' to accomplish same.

Naval officer (30 to 39), Georgia

"People must understand their role in the life process and strive to improve the quality of life for all humanity and not just for those who are of primary concern to them."

I would define the aim of life as the attempt to align our beliefs and actions with the will of God and the example He sent us in Jesus Christ. I believe that if we as businessmen could love and trust each other as Christ taught, then our country would be a much better place to live and work in. It is difficult for a person to conduct his business in an honest and open way if he thinks that everyone is out to get him or cheat him. I believe that a good part of the American business institution has this attitude of dishonesty and distrustfulness.

Treasurer (30 to 39), road construction company, Indiana

The aim of life has to encompass the religious and spiritual sphere. As I grow older and climb the ladder in my vocation, I become more acutely aware of the necessity of God and His guidance in our lives. Problems, tensions, and anxiety promote—at least for me—a feeling of helplessness and lack of purpose. I find that as I seek God and ask His help, there develops a sense of purpose in my life. Surely the aim of life must be related in large part to the Creator and to what He proposes for us and as He relates it to us.

Senior vice president (30 to 39), Texas bank

The aim of life is to make the world a better place to live in not only for yourself and family but for all mankind. This would be for the existing generation as well as for future generations. Every man, in evaluating his own personal development, plans, and goals, should tailor them to fit this main purpose of existence.

Marketing manager (30 to 39), chemical manufacturing company, Ohio

The aim of life is not a single objective, but means to me the pursuing of meaningful objectives in several areas such as work, family life, personal relationships, and religion.

Staff manager (30 to 39), financial services organization, North Carolina

The aim of life is to glorify God and to serve Him forever. One does this on earth by serving others—both freely and for profit. Those to be served are the people circumstances place under your charge or in your market. The service to be provided is what is needed as qualified by one's providential and economic capability to meet the need.

Investment officer (30 to 39), private foundation, New York

The aim of life is to enhance the quality of it for others. By helping our brothers and sisters to move toward the achievement of happiness, we are accomplishing what I believe is our raison d'être. There must be a reason for our existence on this planet and for the need for the companionship of and the interaction with others. Each of us has a talent or skill which is uniquely his or her own. It is apparent to me that a Supreme Being with an intellect incalculable to us has designed a world in such a way that we human beings have been given the gift of reason, certain talents, and the right and power to use them to better the condition of our fellows. In so serving others, our own lives are coincidentally enriched in like measure.

It therefore pleases me to see the renewed interest of our young people in the "helping professions." Helping takes on many characteristics. Some of our fellow inhabitants of this planet are almost totally dependent on others for survival. Others have limited ability to be independent, while still others have intellectual capacities and skills in great abundance. It is appropriate that man give of himself in a manner equal to that with which nature has endowed him. By this I mean not that it is necessary that we provide all of the necessities of life for all people, but that we help others to achieve self-actualization. No matter what our talents or capabilities, we can and should do this.

Dietician, program and research director (40 to 49), Pennsylvania university

The aim of life is striving to achieve results or goals of long-term value. Success cannot be measured in terms of results alone, but in terms of the quality and the manner in which one strives. Quality and manner should evidence growth toward mature, participative, and ethical characteristics. People must understand their role in the life process and strive to improve the quality of life for all humanity and not just for those who are of primary concern to them.

Purchasing manager (40 to 49), chemical company, Pennsylvania

To find contentment and happiness should be the aim of life. Each individual will be content and happy with different things. There is no universal "aim."

Vice president (40 to 49), electronics company, California

The conscious evolution of the total human being—physical, emotional, mental, and spiritual.

President (40 to 49), home building company, Colorado

The aim of life is to provide for the safety and health of the family and to fill the days with work and other interesting activities in "comfortable" economic circumstances.

Management consultant (40 to 49), accounting firm, Pennsylvania

Being created in the image of the Master Creator, we have a responsibility to make a meaningful contribution to the world. This contribution is manifested in that which has gone on before and is yet to come. It is doing the best you can at any and all tasks you undertake, including marriage, occupation, and the rearing of your children. Know yourself, your limitations as well as your assets, and then make the best of both in gaining whatever satisfaction and material things you want in life while making your contribution.

Vice president and director of operations (40 to 49), New York company

The aim of life, as I see it, is the direction a person "wants" to go in. Some people do not do as they want to but go in a direction other people want them to go in. Thus they become unhappy in their jobs, family life, and in life in general. Once people learn to enjoy life by doing what they want to do, they find themselves much happier and much more content.

Administrator (40 to 49), traffic safety program, Texas

In my opinion, the aim of life is to create an atmosphere around yourself so that everyone who comes into contact with you can be made happier in one way or another as a result.

Manager (40 to 49), bakery chain, Illinois

I would define the aim of life as setting out each day to meet the world on its own terms. My interests are greatly concerned with my family, friends, and colleagues. I believe in treating them as human beings and being sensitive to their problems. I also love animals—domestic and wild—and I try to regard all of them as "living creatures" who have a contribution to make to the well-being of us all. People who are insensitive to animals are insensitive to other people. I strive to be known as a humanitarian.

Management consultant (40 to 49), Maryland

Personally, I believe that the aim of life should be to develop a philosophy of living that allows one to adapt to change in oneself and one's environment—a philosophy too that exalts life's intangibles such as honesty, integrity, love, and genuine feelings of good will for one's fellow men. I further believe that we should all aim to become physically, spiritually, psychologically, and emotionally mature. We should all seek to achieve internal peace and external compatibility with all facets of our environment.

Director of administration (50 to 59), state agency, Virginia

We have a tremendous heritage in our country. Millions of Americans have laid their lives on the line in previous generations to protect our way of life and our right to self-determination. To fulfill our heritage and to preserve it for future generations, I believe that each one of us has a responsibility to utilize whatever God-given talents we may have to make our communities, our state, and our nation a better place to live and work. This is the message I feel we must tell and sell to the youth of today.

Chief executive officer (50 to 59), electric distribution cooperative, Colorado

The best definition I know of the aim of life comes from a quotation ascribed to Elbert Hubbard: "I wish to be simple, honest, natural, frank, clean in mind and body, unaffected—ready to say, 'I do not know,' if it be—to meet all men on an absolute equality—to face any obstacle and meet every difficulty unafraid and unabashed. I wish to live without hate, whim, jealousy, envy, or fear. I wish others to live their lives, too—up to their highest, fullest, and best. To that end I pray that I may never meddle, dictate, interfere, give advice that is not wanted, nor assist when my services are not needed. If I can help people, I will do it by giving them a chance to help themselves; and

if I can uplift or inspire, let it be by example, inference and suggestion, rather than by injunction and dictation. I desire to radiate life."

President (50 to 59), electronics manufacturing company, Texas

The aim of life is to understand the "who," "what," "when," "where," and "how" of my life and to be truthful and sincere in my actions and self-appraisal. The aim of life is to make an effort to recognize my strengths and to correct my weaknesses.

Vice president, finance (50 to 59), petroleum products exploration and production company, Texas

To me, the aim of life is to achieve self-satisfaction by contributing to social and technological progress and the perpetuation of the human race.

Director and treasurer (50 to 59), psychological research organization, Virginia

The aim of life is the attainment of self-satisfaction and a peaceful conscience. One attains these by developing the ability to love and to be loved, by developing the need for and the capability to work (produce goods or services), by exploring the unknown, by providing a legacy, and by preparing for life after death.

Personnel director (50 to 59), insurance company, Oregon

127

"My philosophy for the 'aim of life' is that we are put on earth for one purpose—to make the world a better place for someone else to live in."

My philosophy for the "aim of life" is that we are put on earth for one purpose—to make the world a better place for someone else to live in. One of my disappointments with the American way of life is that I was taught Horatio Alger morals but have found that people and our business institutions do not abide by these. Instead both follow the code that "the ends justify the means." Business, rather than doing a self-examination to identify its failures to contribute to the American way of life, would rather cast aspersions on "productivity." Also, the younger generation, because it has never been without food, clothing, and shelter, is not motivated to "drive" as hard as those of us born in the 1920s and 1930s.

Director of physical plant (50 to 59), Michigan university

To me, the aim of life is the development of talents and personal potential. If this can be done, then the other criteria for "success" will be achieved as a byproduct of this process. The primary hindrance to achievement in society (any society) and to the development of talents and personal potential is one's attitude. Attitude is the determining factor. With due allowance for the unfortunate souls who are emotionally or mentally crippled and who cannot achieve even the bare minimum of performance in our present society, I believe the above holds true for the vast majority of people operating in our society. Most people operate at 20 percent or less of their possible performance level in terms of personal abilities. Most vastly underrate themselves and their ability to achieve. One of the most crippling forces limiting performance in our society is attitude which is clouded by emotional immaturity.

Sales manager (50 to 59), optical supplies company, Ohio

My basic belief is that we are all here on this earth to assist one another in obtaining eternal life after death. Therefore, I would like to direct my life so that I will be assisting others and myself to this final goal. If I fail, then I will be depriving others of the assistance to which they are entitled.

Director of continuing education (60 or over), Colorado hospital

The aim of life is the desire to improve oneself and one's surroundings by actively participating in life. Too many people today succumb to the emotional preference of the comfortable solution instead of the difficult one. It is easy to do nothing. It is easy to concentrate on attacking the symptoms and seeking short-term placebos. It is not easy—but much more important—to review the world as a whole and to define and ensure the conditions for its improvement as well as its survival. The critical issue is not what we know but what we do. The great end in life is not knowledge but action.

Administrative officer (60 or over), federal government agency, California

The aim of life is to discover the purpose that lies at its heart and then to give your best toward achieving that purpose. To me this means acknowledging a divine will whose purposes are benevolent and loving for all creation—a divine will who calls forth from me a response that is benevolent and loving for all. Out of this response flows the truly meaningful satisfactions in life—a sense of meaning, self-respect, respect for others, integrity, fulfillment, peace of heart and mind, confidence that life's worthwhileness is not dependent on the satisfaction of all physical and material wants.

Agency director (60 or over), New Jersey

I have reached the conclusion that the aim of life (the only one that seems to me to stand the test of time) is to have children and to teach them and prepare them as best you can to lead their own lives. How do we do this? First, give them a good education, and, second, teach them right from wrong. This we must do ourselves. This responsibility cannot be delegated.

Marketing manager (60 or over), industrial manufacturing company, Michigan

My definition of the aim of life is twofold. First, the aim of life is to achieve as much as possible during our lifetime in terms of self-fulfillment and service to the human community. Second, the aim of life is to prepare as thoroughly as possible for the next epoch—whatever that may be.

Treasurer (60 or over), wholesale distribution company, California

The aim of life is to try to apply the Golden Rule—to love, to appreciate, to at least like your neighbor. The aim of life is to try to change things for the better, to avoid hurting another person, and to comfort those who have been hurt.

Hospital administrator (40 to 49), California